THE
SINGLE
WOMAN'S
BLUEPRINT

STOP CHASING A MAN
START CHASING YOUR DREAMS

MONICA ALMOND

ZION
PUBLISHING HOUSE

Los Angeles   Washington, DC

© 2018 by Monica Almond

Library of Congress Control Number 2018909419

Published by ZION Publishing House
Los Angeles & Washington, D. C.
www.zionpublishinghouse.com

Monica Almond
The Single Woman's Blueprint: STOP Chasing a Man. START Chasing Your Dreams.

ISBN 978-1-7323520-1-8 (pbk.)
ISBN 978-1-7323520-2-5 (ebk.)
ISBN 978-1-7323520-3-2 (hdbk)

Scripture quotations marked TPT are from The Passion Translation®. Copyright © 2017, 2018 by Passion & Fire Ministries, Inc. Used by permission. All rights reserved. ThePassionTranslation.com.

Scripture taken from the Holy Bible, NEW INTERNATIONAL VERSION®, NIV® Copyright © 1973, 1978, 1984, 2011 by Biblica, Inc.® Used by permission. All rights reserved worldwide.

Scripture quotations taken from the Amplified® Bible (AMPC), Copyright © 1954, 1958, 1962, 1964, 1965, 1987 by The Lockman Foundation. Used by permission. www.Lockman.org

Scripture taken from the New King James Version®. Copyright © 1982 by Thomas Nelson. Used by permission. All rights reserved.

Taken from the HOLY BIBLE: EASY-TO-READ VERSION © 2014 by Bible League International. Used by permission.

Some names and details have been changed to protect the privacy of the individuals involved.

Dedication

To Justice, the Giant, and all of the brilliant and beautiful Queens developing. My prayer is that you will own your worth, recognize your power, and chase after your dreams.

Contents

Introduction

Your purpose for life is not found in between the sheets.

A man does not give your life meaning. He won't fulfill your every desire. Your life won't be better because of him. Your purpose is not found in him.

Your purpose is found in God.

You have picked up a book that will categorically change your perspective on who you are as a woman. If you are a believer, this book will alter your perspective on who you are as a woman of God. You are extraordinarily valuable to God. So valuable, that He saved the best for last when He formed you out of man. Because God is perfect, He knew that man would need you to fulfill his purpose in the earth. You are more valuable than society, past relationships, and even the church have led you to believe.

The narrative in this book is a testament to God's Grace and His Mercy. Grace and Mercy are an inseparable pair. Like me, I'm sure you're comfortably acquainted with them both. God's grace is His indwelling power that allows you and me to operate outside of our own limited human ability. The grace of God enables you to handle and survive tests and situations that you would not normally be able to handle on your own, if it were not for God's intervening power. I survived (overcame and recovered from) many failed relationships by God's grace as documented through many experiences in this book.

God's mercy—His unmerited favor toward us, is what He bestowed upon me when He gave me a second chance. It was more like an umpteenth chance, as I was so foolish, ignorant, and naive on my journey of singleness that I often returned to the hot stove to burn myself over and over and over again. But, my Heavenly Father never failed to pick me up, brush me off, wipe my tears, and remind me how much He loved me, still wanted to bless me, and give me more than I could ever dream, imagine, or conceive despite my many faults. He longs to do the same for you.

No matter where you currently reside in the game of life, I know you have been bumped from your position a few times. I know you have had your heart broken—in some cases, many times. I know you are sick and tired of giving your heart to the wrong man, only to suffer a crushing disappointment. I know you have lain in your bed awake at night, crying your eyes out and asking God, "Why is this happening to me?" "You said You wouldn't give me more than I can bear, and I certainly can't bear this!" Hear me when I say I've been there, many times, which is why I wrote this book.

What God has placed on my heart to share with you in this book, He first allowed in my life. My life was once void and without purpose. Then, I allowed the Creator of the universe to mold my heart, to change my thinking, and to show me my purpose. Once I had suffered enough heartbreak, I finally surrendered my all to God! I stopped putting all of my energy chasing after a man and a relationship, and I redirected that energy to chasing my dream. But, you don't have to wait as long as I did.

You must understand God's plan for you is bigger than begging a man for his attention, being the other woman, or settling for less than what you deserve. Let me reiterate, **God's plan for you is bigger than begging a man for his attention, being the other woman, or settling for less than what you deserve.** Your purpose is wrapped up inside of you—the God in you—not inside of an external relationship. Give your life completely and uninhibitedly over to the Father. Allow Him to do in you what He did in me.

First, you must settle it in your mind that God has something greater for you. Something bigger than you could ever conceive in your inadequate earthly mind. God said, "I know what I'm doing. I have it all planned out—plans to take care of you, not abandon you, plans to give you the future you hope for." Jeremiah 29:11 (The Message Bible).

I am completely transparent in this book—about my own experiences in relationships and that of others. I don't intend to sugar-coat real issues that women struggle with every day, particularly women in the church. Believe it or not, Christian women deal with crises, such as extramarital affairs, pre-marital sex, abuse, and three-way relationships, just like other women who may not openly profess their salvation. These issues are very much alive and tearing through scores of churches and households around the world. Why aren't we talking about them? Are we afraid to talk about infidelity in the church? I mean like really talk about it, to the point where men and women share their experiences of hurt and shame from the pulpit, which can lead to someone being delivered right in the church. How powerful would that be? We are ineffective for the Kingdom if we are still bound by our own sin, shame, hurt, and guilt.

I may be unorthodox at times by what I share, but God did not call me to this work to hand-hold. Real issues require real solutions, and my prayer is that you will find tangible solutions within the pages of this book, regardless if you profess faith or not.

I have been on a journey of self-discovery for a very long time. Even as I write these words, I am learning more and more about myself—the way I love, the way I receive love, and the way I view relationships. I have read a reasonable number of books on relationships. I read book after book about *How to Get a Man, How to Keep a Man, How to Love a Man, How to Use Your Power as a Woman, Finding Your Boaz*, and the list goes on and on. But, I have yet to read a book which is concrete, clear, specific, unadulterated, and painstakingly honest about a single woman's identity in Christ and the intense and complicated journey that she navigates toward living a life of purpose, and ultimately marriage—from a woman's perspective that is.

My prayer is that this book empowers you, encourages you, gives you hope, and most of all, SETS YOU FREE! So, the chains of delusion, fear, loneliness, emptiness, sadness, despair, unworthiness, and rejection permanently fall from your life. So, you can finally see the road ahead and do what God has created you to do in the earth. **God's desire for you is that you would let go of your past, discover your purpose, and pursue your dreams.** Come along with me on this journey, Sis. You got this. Better yet, God's got this!

About the "Elevation" sections:

There is a section called Elevation at the end of each of the five parts in this book. If you have purchased the workbook in addition to the book, there are additional prompts to complete and activities to engage in. These Elevation sections are intended to elevate your thinking and bring you to and through your place of healing and restoration, into a life of purpose. Take advantage of these prompts and do what they ask. Completing the prompts in the order in which they are written will allow you to experience the full utility of this book and the freedom it offers. Don't just read this book passively but actively engage in it and participate in what it asks you to do. You picked up this book because you want results—go after them.

Part I: Embrace Your Singleness

I want you to close your eyes and picture yourself standing alone on the shore of your favorite beach. You're standing there looking into the vastness of the ocean, and it's just you and the waves tossing back and forth, crashing onto the rocks. As your eyes focus on the expanse of the waters, you feel someone grab you and thrust you into the water. The next thing you know, you're going deeper and deeper into the water, gasping trying to catch your breath. You make an attempt to release yourself from the hold of your captor and push your way back to the surface, to no avail. Eventually, you find yourself on the ocean floor yet perfectly conscious.

After you get over the shock of still being alive, you pick yourself up from the bottom of the ocean to meet Jesus standing there with His arms open wide. Jesus calls you by name, extends His arms further, and grabs you in the most loving embrace. Your knees get weak, your legs give out, and you begin to sob uncontrollably, as Jesus catches you. He holds you even tighter and closer and begins to tell you how much He loves you, and that He has been waiting on this encounter with you since the day you were born. He then grabs you by the hand and leads you through what appears to be a motion picture showing scenes from your life—past, present, and future. Many of the images bring you great joy, but there are images that recount past sorrows. Scenes that cause you great pain and turmoil. Some of the scenes are you growing up without a father, or with a father who was too busy to notice. Some scenes are of you living a rebellious and carefree lifestyle, giving your heart and your body away to men who were not worthy of either. Scenes of you being rejected, heart-broken by people you trusted, being used and manipulated, even raped, and abused.

You begin to feel tears welling up in your eyes as you recall the many nights of heartache, confusion, frustration, anger, fear, loneliness, and pain. Jesus stands in front of you, wipes the tears from your eyes, and presents you with a gift. You look up and meet Jesus' eyes in bewilderment. "Why would Jesus be giving me a gift?" you say to yourself. "I'm not worthy of His gift". Reluctantly, you begin to unwrap the gift and find that the gift is Jesus' heart. Jesus presents you with His heart. You stand there dumbfounded. "Why would Jesus give me His heart?" 'Who am I, you ask yourself, that Jesus would consider me worthy enough to deserve His heart?' Hearing your thoughts, Jesus leans over and says, "My heart is an expression of My undying love for you. I've loved you before the foundation of the world, and My love for you will never end." Then, Jesus shows you a vision of the rest of your life. The next scenes include you living a life full of purpose. Instead of carrying around the dead weight of your past, you see yourself beginning to dream again, to live again, and to truly value the life you've been given. You see yourself experiencing something you've never encountered—unspeakable joy! The scene ends.

God created you and me to live a life of purpose. As the previous scene depicts, God doesn't hold our sins against us, but simply wants us to embrace His love, so we can go about doing everything He's called us to do. God is constantly reminding us how much He loves us, and that we find our meaning in Him not in relationships. This chapter begins to debunk the many myths associated with the world's view on single living. I introduce to you the single woman and the many facets of her life—from the ups and downs of being single and the kind of emotion that it stirs—loneliness, fear, and anger—to the challenges of being a single mother, a single Black woman, and fighting the stigmas associated with each characterization. I also talk about the importance of fighting off loneliness, and how loneliness can and will cause a single woman to compromise her core values.

God created you and me to live a life of purpose.

These are all real issues women all around the world face each and every day—whether they are married or single, Black or White, rich or poor, religious or irreligious. Like the rest of this book, the purpose of this first chapter is to cause you to reprogram the way that you identify with your singleness. Rather than seeing singleness as a curse or a forgotten existence—one that lacks relevance and appreciation—see it as a launching pad into your dreams and the core of who God made you to be. Embrace your singleness. There is a purpose in this season. Rest assured. God knows exactly what He's doing. Give Him the permission to steer your life.

The Single Struggle is Real

Being a single woman can be a very enjoyable experience. When you're single and void of attachments, you're free to manage your own time, money, and decisions without the need for a second opinion. Singleness is a time for self-discovery. It's a time to explore the life path God has called you to. Many people complete some form of higher education while they're single, kick-start a business, or launch off into a career, buy their first home, travel, and truly experience life in an attempt to identify with themselves and with the world around them. There are many things to learn and benefit from during this exploratory phase of your life.

What's important to remember along your single journey, is that your period of singleness is only for a season—if you desire to get married that is. Also, during your season of singleness, your life should be completely and wholly devoted to God. It means that rather than ministering to the needs of your husband, you are ministering to God, and God is ministering to you. When you're single you don't have the competing interests of serving your spouse and serving God—you can be completely and entirely devoted to God. See I Corinthians 7:34-35. Every waking thought is on God—you ponder Him, consider Him, desire Him, meditate on what to say to Him and how to spend your time in His presence. Being single has plenty of rewards, if you recognize and take advantage of them.

But, let's be real—being a single, **Christian woman,** ain't easy! There are no shortage of challenges that single Christian women must endure on a daily basis. One of the biggest threats to fend off is temptation. Temptation is synonymous with destruction. Synonymous with, "You should have said 'NO!' when you had the chance!" Simply put, temptation can alter the course of your life, and if you aren't careful, can lead you down a path to complete destruction where five/ten/twenty years later you're coming up for air wondering what happened and where all the time went. Believe me when I say I am a living witness.

For the majority of my single life, I was carefree (i.e.) careless, foolish, gullible, ignorant, naive, stupid, [insert pitiful adjective here] about who I dated, what I drank, what I smoked, and even who I slept with. The enemy had a willing and able vessel in me. I was not operating under the moral code I was taught as a little girl and had no one to blame for my poor decision-making but myself. The Word of God says in James 1:13-15, "When tempted, no one should say, 'God is tempting me.' For God cannot be tempted by evil, nor does he tempt anyone; but each person is tempted when they are dragged away by their own evil desire and enticed. Then, after desire has conceived, it gives birth to sin; and sin, when it is full-grown, gives birth to death." (New International Version)

When you allow a thought to form in your mind, and you begin to meditate on that thought—it moves from your mind to your heart. Once it's in your heart, you have your mind made up. Now, you act on that original thought. This is a place I found myself in over and over again. All it took was a suggestion from the enemy to get me to believe that what I was considering doing but had not yet made a decision about doing, was normal and appropriate—completely ignoring the perfect will of the Holy Spirit.

The power of suggestion is a destructive force, and the enemy will bring evil desires to your mind so subtly. Initially, they'll be quick thoughts that enter your mind and leave. But, if you don't immediately get control of those thoughts and bring them into captivity and total submission to God's Word, which is His will—the suggestions will open the door to temptation, which then immediately and irrevocably leads you into sin. (II

Corinthians 10:5). **However,** we serve a faithful and a merciful God, Who will rescue us from our own pile of poop and give us another chance to make a mid-course correction. He is a loving God, full of grace and mercy, and He wants to see us win in every area of our lives. When we win, God wins.

The Single Black Female's Struggle is Really Real

Just to be clear, this book was written for ALL women. God is not a respecter of persons and neither am I. However, because I am a Black woman, I would be remiss if I did not address the many challenges inherent with being a single Black female, particularly in the United States. The stigmas and stereotypes are boundless—and the generational impact has been significant.

Survey data reveal that Black women are the least-valued of all women when it comes to relationships, which can make it all the more difficult for a Black woman to marry. According to a Cornell University sociologist, Black women are typically ranked at the bottom of dating preferences on online dating sites. Black women are considered to be at the bottom of the food chain, in general. We are paid less, hired less, and promoted less than our male and female peers. Dating back to slavery, our bodies were treated as objects, and we were used however the slave master saw fit. The Black men who loved us had no power and no control over the dominance of the slave master. If the slave master wanted to rape us, he could because we were his property to be raped, beaten, tormented, and even murdered. We bore our husband's children and our slave master's children. We weren't afforded the time or space to reconcile the trauma emotionally, spiritually, or physically. This is one of the great tragedies of our time.

I won't make you suffer through the litany of counterproductive and fear-inducing heresies and myths associated with Black women, but the dynamics that these issues present work contrary to the development, well-being, and sustainability of this unique demographic. Add onto this dynamic, the reality of the percentage of Black women who have never been married, and the picture appears bleak and almost hopeless. According to research, Black women are twice as likely as White women to have never been married[i]. The chances for highly educated Black women to marry have declined for a number of reasons. One, there is a significant disparity in education between Black women and Black men. When Black women comprise 71% of Black graduate students, if they are in search of a highly educated Black man, they are in for a rude awakening. Further, highly educated Black men are more willing to marry outside of their race than highly educated Black women, which further reduces the chances of an educated Black woman marrying a Black man with comparable credentials.

And, finally, as facts have long depicted, Black men are in

prison at disproportionate rates. In 2014, 516,900 Black men were imprisoned in comparison with 22,600 Black women[ii]. With this in mind, as a Black woman it is absolutely critical you have confidence in who you are and with whom God may be calling you to in marriage. He may not be calling you to marry a Black man. God may be trying to get you to expand your horizons or to relax unrealistic expectations in order to lead you to an experience you would have never dreamed of. Just make sure your heart is in the right place, and the criteria that you have identified for your mate are truly the qualities that God has placed on your heart. I would hate for you to miss your blessing. If for you, living in God's fullness at some point includes marriage, take an inventory of your life and your expectations for a mate and compare them against what the Holy Spirit is revealing to you about marriage.

The Single Mother IS NOT the Weakest Link

The single mother has a very unique experience when dating. It is a myth however, to believe that the single mother is the weakest link in the dating game. Single mothers have several powerful attributes from the experience of raising children that make them uniquely qualified to partner in marriage and maintain an orderly household. I say that because I've been a single mother for fifteen years.

I do want to be clear about what my personal definition of a single mother is. Though they come in a variety of forms, some mothers experience raising their children truly by themselves. My definition of a "single mother" is a mother who is relationally single according to society's definition—essentially not married. She is also a woman who has no support from the child's father or the support that she does have is extremely limited. Some women identify themselves as single mothers if they are simply single (not married) and mothers—but the child's father is still a very active part of their lives, either physically, financially or both. These two scenarios make for very different experiences. For more than a decade I fell into the first category. During that time, I experienced a host of tumultuous encounters with men that now when I look back, I realize they saw my single motherhood as an extreme weakness and chose to capitalize on my vulnerability. Unfortunately, I was the one who put this self-destructive pattern in motion. Let me explain.

When I was twenty-one years old, I was a student at a world-renowned historically Black university. This university perpetuates an atmosphere of empowerment and progression and is a place where students who are lucky enough to attend engage in bold, controversial, and critical dialogue about issues which impact them and the world around them. Students who enroll at this university leave more confident about who they are as members of the African diaspora, more empowered as individuals, and more determined about their place as global citizens.

This institution did all of that for me, but where I got it wrong was when I started making bold declarations like, "I would be fine as a single mother." I said this because I thought I was so smart, independent, and capable of building and sustaining my own earthly legacy. That is not the takeaway the university's pioneering faculty and scholars had in mind when they were chartering new courses to embolden and empower future Black scholars and leaders. But, I was foolish. I was not at a place where I had awareness about the power of my words. The Word of God is clear when it says, "Death and life are in the power of the tongue: and they that love it shall eat the fruit thereof" Proverbs 18:21 (King James Version). The Bible also states that a man can set the course of his life on fire with his tongue. (James 3:6). With those words, I spoke my situation into existence. I effectively declared the outcome of my situation which resulted in my subsequent pregnancy, a successive and tumultuous relationship with my daughter's father, and a daughter who lived most of her formative years without the regular presence of a father. When I uttered these foolish words, I was in no way considering the consequences that would result and how much my life, but more importantly my daughter's life, would be impacted.

But thanks be to God, who restores, and forgives, and Who gave me a second chance! When you come to God boldly and with a humble and repentant heart, He hears you, and He can reverse the course of your life, essentially invalidating the mess you created. Aren't you glad about it? What God has done for me, He can do for you. Whatever words you've spoken that you wish you could take back—whether it has to do with your relationships, your finances, your family, or your career, just repent from those words. Pray this prayer:

> Father God, I repent of the words that I spoke that did not align with your perfect will for my life. I ask that you would invalidate those words now so that they will have no effect in my life or in the lives of those they may be impacting now. I replace those words with Your Word that gives life and not death. Your Word that says that everything I put my hands to do shall prosper! Your Word that says I am above only and never beneath, I am the head and not the tail! Your Word that says no weapon formed against me shall prosper! So, right now I declare that not even the weapon of my former foolish words will prosper against me and take root in my life. I thank You in advance for changing the course of my life and causing it to line up with your perfect will, in Jesus Name, Amen!

Don't Believe the Hype
Now, don't get it twisted. There are some single mother tendencies that paint a bad image of single mothers. Entertainment helps to play a role in that. Take the women that we spend hours fantasizing over on "reality

television", who are constantly at odds with their "baby's daddies". These women who appear to have it all because they either married or slept with a famous athlete, rapper, producer, hypeman, or the like. How they entered the relationship is of no consequence—the point is they are no longer with their sperm donor, and yet they continue to reap the "benefits" (AKA, child support) of said relationship, which results in these delusional women flaunting their lifestyles on television, exacerbating false expectations to the masses. As believers, rather than condoning their behavior by being devout followers of these shows and allowing debilitating language and imagery to seep into our spirits, we should refuse to contribute to the ratings and allow these shows to fail, miserably.

The **real** reality this lifestyle brings is more grim than what you might catch on the latest "housewives" show. The children that result from these relationships may look like they **have it all** on TV, but these are the same children we see in tabloids years later with drug abuse problems and felony convictions. The real deal is, daughters who grow up without fathers in the household are more likely to be promiscuous, become teen mothers, and have children out of wedlock, than daughters whose fathers are a constant presence in their lives. Sons whose fathers are absent are more likely to be suspended and expelled from school and more likely to end up with one or more encounters with the justice system, than young men whose fathers are active in their lives. The statistics bear this out.

Children who grow up with only one biological parent are 40% less likely to graduate from high school and are less likely to attend college than children raised by two parents. Children who are raised without a father present have more behavior problems than children with a father present.

The statistics for children who are raised by single Black mothers are devastating. Fifty percent of Black children under eighteen years of age live in a household which is headed by a single mother—more than double that of Whites (19%), leading to a number of unpleasant outcomes [iii]. The official poverty rate in 2013 for households headed by single Black women was 46% in comparison with 12% for Black two-parent households.[iv]

Being a single parent significantly affects your pocketbook. As a single mother, you are more likely to be poor than well off. Pause and think about that. Don't underestimate the effects that poorly informed decisions, impulse, and untamed emotion can have on your children and your lifestyle. What reasonable parent wants the very least for their child? Don't get caught up in the false hype of what this world tells you is glamorous about single motherhood. The reality is, children need their fathers. That should go without saying.

Also, know, that being a child of God means that all of the statistics I've laid out here do not have to apply to you. Once you receive revelation on who you are and the fact that you were bought with a price and that Jesus already paid the penalty of sin and death on your behalf, effectively assuming all your sin, guilt, and inferiority—you no longer have to live according to the standards and statistics of the world. You are now governed by the Gospel of Grace. My advice to you is to grab a hold of the Word and inhale it until you become the reality of what God created you to be. You and your children don't have to be a statistic.

First Thing's First

It's unfortunate that I have to cover this, but sadly this happens more often than not. While you are still a single woman and before you say, "I do" to your new beau, your children are still your number one priority. Of course, your priorities shift once you get married, and your marriage rightfully takes center stage, but while dating and before you tie the knot, your children take priority. So, DO NOT put a man before your children!!! Your children were there before that fine specimen of a man showed up, and they require your time and attention even once he arrives, and in some cases, even more so. Should this new love interest not be the man God has chosen for you to marry, you don't want to have to pick up the pieces of your relationships with your children, having neglected them while exhausting your emotional and physical energy on a man. Your children need to know that just because a man has shown up on the scene, it does not mean your love for them has shifted or downgraded. If nothing else, they should experience twice the love because of your significant other.

This shift in thinking was so important to me as I got older and started truly dating for marriage. I wanted my daughter to know I had not forgotten about her, and I still had my finger on the pulse of her world. I made sure my time was not always spent dating and away from her, but that I balanced my time well between getting to know someone new and continuing to deepen my relationship with her. There were many years where I was not as intentional and neglected my daughter's needs considerably. The fruit of that neglect began to materialize in certain behaviors and patterns, that now looking back, I would have gone about things much differently. The neglect though was not always the result of being in a relationship, sometimes it was a result of my ambitions and my passions—though admirable, they were in direct conflict with the time and attention my daughter needed—especially since I was the only physical parent she had.

Loneliness is Dangerous

Many women find it hard to embrace their singleness because for some, being single means being alone. Many women fight loneliness—particularly single mothers, divorced women, and women who are accustomed to being in long-term or multiple relationships. Loneliness however, is a choice, just like being bored is a choice. People choose to be lonely, they choose to be bored, they even choose to be depressed. Actively setting your mind on something positive takes work. I'm sure at some point in your life you were infatuated with a man so much that you actively and purposefully went out of your way to engage him, even relentlessly pursue him—because you wanted him that badly. He consumed your mind and your thoughts so much that you meditated on being together with him. Well, all of the energy you put into pursuing that man, you could have put into being content in the presence of God, waiting on Him to fulfill your desires and occupying any lonely place in your heart.

Do you honestly believe God's intention is for you to end up with junk? God wants to give you more than you could ever think, dream, wish, hope or desire. He wants to blow your mind! The book of Ephesians, Chapter 3, verse 20, the Amplified Bible, Classic Edition says it plainly, "Now to Him Who, by (in consequence of) the [action of His] power that is at work within us, is able to [carry out His purpose and] do superabundantly, far over and above all that we [dare] ask or think [infinitely beyond our highest prayers, desires, thoughts, hopes, or dreams].

Waiting for your Boaz requires you to completely surrender your will and desire for a mate to God. God is perfect, remember? He doesn't make mistakes. He's not going to mess up and send you the wrong mate. After He created the universe by speaking it into existence on the 6th day, God stood back, admired His creative product, and said, "This is some good stuff!" He didn't say, "Wait a minute. I think I messed up with the light. I should not have called light, DAY. I should have called light, NIGHT." No, EVERYTHING God created was perfect! There were no do-overs. Because He is not capable of making mistakes, He is not capable of revisions, alterations, or reenactments. HE IS GOD! So, take Him at His word when He tells you He will give you the desires of your heart.

I know several women who would rather be in a relationship with a man they know is not good for them than to be alone. Debbie, a good friend of mine, began a long-term relationship while she was still in high school. Debbie's boyfriend became her world, and she became his. They adopted each other's families, spent holidays together, and were as "thick as thieves." Debbie remained in a monogamous relationship with this man for nearly seven years. Even after they lived apart for many years to pursue their own endeavors, they remained committed. Everyone expected the two of them to marry—Debbie included. But, Debbie's long-term boo was not ready to propose. Debbie could not understand why he was not ready to take the next step when they had been together for so long. She wanted to partner with him and grow their lives together. He had other plans.

Once that relationship ended, Debbie started dating again, but she adopted a different philosophy. She loved hard, but she simply chose to settle for whatever a man was willing to give her. She convinced herself that whatever the man wanted, she wanted. If the man told her he did not want to be in a relationship but was willing to spend all of his time over her house, stay the night, and assume all of the benefits of a husband, she convinced herself that she, too, was okay with that. Debbie was living in denial. All the while she was being torn apart inside because she became complacent and compromised her desires, ultimately silencing her true feelings. Her desperation to feel loved and needed led her to lose herself in the process.

As women, we crave love and attention. We actually need it. It's part of our genetic make-up to receive the love of a man and to feel the safety and security that comes from being in a mutually-reinforcing relationship. When we don't feel like we're getting our needs met in a relationship, and if we don't have a firm grasp on who we are, we eventually relinquish control of our true desires and simply settle for whatever morsels or crumbs that are swept onto the floor. Any ounce of attention or devotion that a man is willing to throw our way, we stand at the ready. This behavior is toxic and often leads to extramarital affairs and three-way relationships, which I cover later in Part III.

The moment you relinquish control of your authority as a woman is the moment you relinquish control of your life. Period. You are the captain of your own ship with the Word of God and The Holy Spirit as your compass. Jesus left us The Holy Spirit to lead us and guide us into all truth. Make full use of The Holy Spirit that lives on the inside of you and avoid the pitfalls that are so common among women who are needy, delusional, and desperate. But, don't beat yourself up if you find yourself in this situation—we've all been there. Make it your mission not to stay there.

You must know who you are before you can enter into a relationship that will have any potential for success. God created you in His image and His likeness. You are a masterpiece! Part V covers this in greater depth, but to put it plainly, **if you fail to recognize the qualities and the power God has put on the inside of you, don't expect a man to.** Good men are attracted to women who give off an aroma of self-confidence, purpose, and self-love not women who smell desperate, needy, and destitute. Smell yourself. What do you smell like? If it's a repugnant and nauseating smell, chances are other people smell the same thing, and it's time for you to change your drawers.

It's never too late to pull yourself out of a pit no matter your age or the number of relationships you've experienced. Don't allow loneliness to cause you to lose sight of who you are and Whose you are. **Singleness is not a curse; it is a temporary calling.** Use it to your advantage and leverage it to God's glory. And, never, ever, ever give up on yourself. Never give up on God, and never give up on love. After all, **God is love, and He will never give up on you.**

Singleness is not a curse; it is a temporary calling.

MAJOR THEMES

- God created you to live a life of purpose.
- You find your meaning in God, not in relationships.
- Enjoy, and yes, embrace your single status. Maximize your time for exploration and adventure and covet your time with God.
- Be open to who God may be calling you to in marriage. The man you need may not come in the package you originally envisioned.
- You set the course of your life with your words. Choose your words wisely.
- As a single mother, keep first things first—your children not your man.
- Do not relinquish control of your life to another human being. Relinquish control to God.
- If you fail to recognize the qualities and the power God has put on the inside of you, don't expect a man to.
- Singleness is not a curse; it is a temporary calling.

ELEVATION

Write a letter to your younger self. If you have a daughter, goddaughter, or a young niece, write a letter addressed to one or each of them. In the letter, share with them what you wish someone would have shared with you about their identity and how to approach dating and relationships as a young girl coming of age.

Part II: Recognize Your Value

"You formed my innermost being, shaping my delicate inside and my intricate outside, and wove them all together in my mother's womb. I thank you, God, for making me so mysteriously complex! Everything you do is marvelously breathtaking. It simply amazes me to think about it! How thoroughly you know me, Lord! You even formed every bone in my body when you created me in the secret place, carefully, skillfully shaping me from nothing to something. You saw who you created me to be before I became me! Before I'd ever seen the light of day, the number of days you planned for me were already recorded in your book."
Psalm 139:13-16 The Passion Translation (TPT)

What would this world look like if all the women in it knew their worth? Would there be an endless amount of unwanted pregnancies and single-parent households? Would there be salty and bitter women raising their daughters to be salty and bitter too? Would there be wounds so deep that women lacked the strength to love again? If all the women in the world understood how God formed them in the Garden, they WOULD NOT settle for second best in anything—in relationships, in business, on their jobs, in their finances, or in leadership roles. You'd have a world full of Esthers, Deborahs, and Ruths. Women who were determined to take hold of everything God had in store for them, reaping ridiculous harvests as a result.

What kind of woman are you? Do you compromise when your flesh gets the best of you, fold to rejection, and lose heart when another year passes with you still being single? Or are you flying high, walking in your purpose, pursuing your dreams, and spending most of your time devoted to your passion, that you barely notice you're still single? What kind of woman are you? Are you a woman that you are proud of?

For many years I was not proud of the woman that I was. I was weak and impressionable. I was desperate and needy. I was rebellious and isolated. I appeared to be on the outside the inverse of what I was on the inside. Living this way is tiring. Having to put on and take off a mask every day will wear anybody out. Ask Catwoman! It's exhausting! More than that, it creates a lonely and depressing environment that only and always attracts the wrong kind of attention from the wrong people.

I will say this over and over and over again: Do not get weary in well doing. **Don't get tired of holding out when a man asks you to put out.** Don't get tired of waiting for the man that God showed you in your vision by settling for the first "saved" man that crosses your path. Don't get tired of providing the response, "I'm single," whenever someone asks your relationship status. And, don't get tired of praying for your future mate. It will all be worth it. If you do it God's way, in His time, after everything has been strategically aligned, you too will walk down the aisle into the arms of the man God preordained for you. But, don't get weary, as you wait.

Don't Compromise to Get or Keep a Man

Being single is not an indictment of your self-worth. When you lower your standards, you lower your worth. Your happiness and your worth as a woman should not be contingent upon whether you are in a relationship. Let me say that again, **your happiness and your worth as a woman should not be contingent upon whether you are in a relationship.** To put it plainly, if your joy and your reason for living and breathing are tied to a man, then your priorities are out of order. If you are not happy before you enter a relationship, being in a relationship is not going to make you happy. Your happiness comes from God not man. I cover this at length in Part IV, "Return to Your First Love."

Many times as women, we quickly let down our guard in relationships and totally forget what life was like before the relationship. We make a vow to ourselves and to God that we won't let a man stay the night, that we won't have sex with him, and that we won't lose sight of the rest of our lives when we enter a relationship. But those promises are quickly broken when we start to "fall in love." We begin to lose sight of our standards and cave in to our emotions and our flesh. You're familiar with the typical patterns. We stand up our friends for our man, neglect church, invite the man into our home at all hours of the night, and put our dreams on hold. Foolishly, we think by doing all these things that eventually our sacrifices and compromises will lead to marriage. Let me tell you, by far on the average, that is not the typical outcome.

Compromising who you are to get and keep a man leads you to a false sense of happiness and fulfillment. I remember reading an article once about Lance Armstrong's first wife. She shared in the article that for her entire adult life she committed her time to supporting Lance by raising his children and supporting his dreams of winning the Tour de France among other prestigious competitions. But, in doing so, she lost who she was in the process. She could no longer identify with the person she saw in the mirror. Unfortunately, (and fortunately) when their marriage ended, she finally started to live. Don't let this be you.

Don't get tired of holding out when a man asks you to put out.

Don't put yourself in the position of wanting to be married so badly that you compromise every part of who God created you to be, just to be with a man and simply to get a ring on your finger. Am I saying that in a marriage, there will not be compromises and sacrifices? Absolutely not. Of course, there will be things you will have to sacrifice in your marriage. But, do not compromise to your detriment. Do not lose sight of your values, your dreams, and your convictions.

Losing sight of who you are is the byproduct of failing to recognize your value in the first place. When you know what you're worth, you don't put anything on the clearance rack, and you don't give away freebies. Whenever you go shopping at popular retail stores like Nordstrom's or Macy's, where do you go to find their clearance items? You certainly won't find any clearance items in the front of the store where the new arrivals are displayed that are worth the most value. You must head to the back of the store to find the items at a reduced rate that are no longer in season. The cheap stuff is always in the back. When a man is shopping for a woman to date and eventually court, he is not looking in the back for a woman who is willing to reduce her value by giving things away. A man who is looking for a wife is looking for a woman up front, with a high price tag who he will have to put in work for. **Every time you compromise your standards, you are reducing the full value of your**

42

assets. This method will not lead to the outcome you are seeking. Trust me—I've been there.

So much of my early dating life was about me trying to navigate through the treacherous dating terrain—and it is treacherous out there! It is particularly hazardous if you are not familiar with certain roadblocks and signs that read, "Do NOT ENTER!", "Stop", and "Slippery when Wet". If I had had even an ounce of common sense, I would have made much better decisions and saved boatloads of time and tears had I paid attention to the manual. Unfortunately, I was too caught up in rebellion to notice, although the signs were staring me right in the face. Thankfully for me, God was building my testimony through it all. Even though I spent years in delusion, those years were not wasted. Rather than living a life of shame, I am sharing my testimony with you and countless other women through this book and through the voice that God has given me to tell His truth. God had a plan for me through all the mistreatment and manipulation that I endured. He has a plan for you, too. But, you must recognize where you are and go about the purification process, so God can truly position you to recognize and receive the marriage He planned for you from the beginning.

Learn to Deal with Rejection

We've all been there. If you have spent any time in a romantic relationship, the odds are you have experienced rejection at least once. You fall for a guy who you are head-over-heels for, spend time investing in a relationship with him or attempting to pursue one, only to be knocked flat on your face with a big, "I don't like you anymore sign" on his forehead. No one likes to experience rejection, but unfortunately it is a part of life. It's what you do with the rejection that determines how you approach your next chapter.

I spent a good portion of my young adult life, acting a plumb fool and sowing my wild oats. Much of this I go into detail about in Part III. Once I finally came to the end of myself, I said, "Enough is enough!" After that long stretch of foolishness—which was from age seventeen to around the age of thirty-three—I got tired. I realized I was on a bridge to nowhere, and I spent several years focused explicitly on seeking the face of the Lord. I went out on a few dates during that time but never ended up in a serious relationship. I knew in my heart I wanted to do things right this time. I recommitted my life to Christ and was intentional about how I spent my time, the images I allowed in my mind, the music I listened to, and the company I kept. The aroma I now gave off as a woman, completely changed. I no longer attracted men with the wrong motives—men who were either intentionally or unintentionally selfish and focused on fulfilling their own needs. I depended on the Holy Spirit to help me to discern the type of man I should engage.

So, when I met Preston, I thought I had struck gold. Preston who served as a deacon at my church found me serving faithfully in ministry. Because he was a deacon, I figured he was adequately vetted, and that I had absolutely nothing to worry about. So, per usual when getting to know someone, we started off just talking on the phone nearly every night. I was inspired by his depth of knowledge in the Word. He KNEW the Word. He could cite every scripture ever written and always provided a biblical context for every circumstance that we discussed—pointing everything back to the Bible, and God's perfect will for our lives. I said, "God, this is a mighty man of valor right here!!!" I was thoroughly intrigued. No man I had ever dated could regurgitate the Word like Him. I just knew this was all the more reason to believe he was "the one."

But there were red flags—which I ignored. But, these weren't the kind of red flags I was used to. I was used to random women calling at random times of the day or lies about a man's marital status. These red flags were camouflaged in self-righteousness. One night, Preston and I had a conversation which he abruptly ended because he didn't like a question I asked him. He called me later in the evening to further express his disdain, and then abruptly ended our relationship. This was truly abnormal behavior to me, since my conversational question was completely harmless, which essentially led to a disagreement about musical preference. I thought to myself, if this is the way this man reacts to small disagreements, how did he ever expect to make it through much more difficult and controversial issues? The very next day however, he called me at work and apologized profusely. He said he was afraid things wouldn't work out with us, so he wanted to end it before either of us got too attached.

So, I dismissed it—after I gave him a run for his money, of course. But, I took him back to my detriment. From that moment on, I almost felt as though I had to tread lightly and disguise who I really was for fear of judgement or rejection from him. I didn't know this then, but I recognize it now. I didn't feel comfortable being my true self with Preston because I knew he wanted a Mother Teresa with a squeaky-clean background. Clearly, I didn't fit the bill! I have been through hell and back in relationships and have done many things that, though I am not proud of them, have made me the woman I am today. Every part of my story is for God's glory. Preston wanted a perfect wife, and fortunately I wasn't her. So, once I finally got naked, (not in the literal sense) and laid everything out on the table, he caved. He chucked up the deuces and bounced. He could not handle my testimony.

I was devastated. How could God present this God-fearing man to me who was an active member in the

church with a heart for the things of God who treated me
like a Queen, to eventually quit on our relationship? I just
knew that the next man God sent my way, since I had
been honoring Him and living for Him, would be my
husband. I was wrong. I was so hurt, confused, and
broken all over again—and by a God-fearing man at that!
Every other man I had dated up until this point was not
really God-fearing, since all they really wanted was the
drawers. So, how could I lose again with a man in the
church?

So. I got down on my knees and cried out to God. I
continued to attend church because I refused to allow my
hurt to keep me from being in the place I needed to be the
most—a house of worship. And, it was painful because he
was at church, and I had to continue to see his face. I had
to watch him serve in the front of the church, and it was
tearing me apart. I could barely stomach it! The enemy
began telling me lies like, "Nobody will ever marry you
because of your past." "You're not worthy of real love."
"You'll never be married." I had to silence the avenger!!!!
Because I serve a God who is full of grace and mercy, He
began to mend my heart and remind me of all the many
blessings He had in store for me. And that not only would
I be married, but that my husband and my marriage would
surpass my wildest dreams!

When rejection comes your way, reflect on the God you
serve and focus on the promises He's given you. He is a

promise-keeping God. You may feel devastated at that moment, but over time, God's love will consume you, and you will only want what He wants. No matter how much you think a man is right for you or how many people you have told that he is the one, God is the ultimate decider. In time, all things will be revealed. Just think about the man He could be saving you *from*! The man you're so "in love" with could be absolutely crazy or prove to be someone else in marriage that leaves you absolutely devastated! Rather than walking away devastated, you should be thanking the fool who is rejecting you! Tell him, "Thank you for not wasting my time. Clearly you ain't the one!" And, keep it movin'!

One final point about dating a "spiritual man" in the church. First, many women are besides themselves to find a man who attends church regularly. The reality is 67% of Christian men do not attend church regularly. Sad, I know, but for now it is what it is. My question to you is, knowing that, why are you waiting for your husband to walk through the church doors? You can sit there and wait, but you may be waiting for the rest of your life. If your husband does happen to walk through those doors, you must still use discernment even—no especially when dating a man in a church. Your spiritual radar DOES NOT go down just because a man goes to church. Just because a man knows the Word does not mean he is spiritually or emotionally equipped to be in a relationship.

And, if a man cannot accept you for who you are, with all the scars you bring with you, SHOW HIM THE DOOR!!

Anyone you are meant to be with will stick around. That is all. Do not force something that should not be. If it is meant to be it will be, and God will give you peace about it. I learned this long ago, "If you doubt, don't." If you don't have peace about a relationship, it is likely not the relationship for you—either right now or at all. So, be still, pay attention to the red flags, and trust God's timing.

> "They went out from us, but they did not really belong to us. For if they had belonged to us, they would have remained with us; but their going showed that none of them belonged to us." I John 2:19 (New International Version).

This is an important reminder about the people in our lives (including exes) who are now gone. They are gone with purpose.

The Pressure of Marriage

Many of us will feel the pressure of marriage at some point, not only from our own families and friends, but from our church family as well. I have lost count of the number of times that people have asked me, "So, Monica are you dating anyone yet?" I am always amazed at their audacity in asking me that question when people can already anticipate my reply which is more often than not, "No, I'm not seeing anyone right now." I am never really sure if they take pleasure in my response being in the negative or if they are truly interested in my well-being.

I received inspiration for this book while I was working on my doctorate degree. I had recently come out of two very trying relationships, both of which I discuss in Part III. I knew that with my history, I had something to say about how to fail in relationships. I'm sure you could also write a book or two about your own experiences. During this time, the Holy Spirit began to show me that I needed to step outside of my comfort zone and relocate back to the East Coast to advance my career and step into the many callings He had ordained for my life. Having already lived in Washington, D.C. when I was an undergraduate student and always having the desire to return, this was not something I had to wrestle a good deal with. I knew my daughter was still young enough, and although she would certainly miss being with her family and friends in California, she would be able to adjust a lot better as an eight-year-old than she would as a teenager. So, after prayer and brief deliberation, I began to make plans to move back to Washington.

In preparing for my move, a few times I was asked, "So, Monica, are you moving because you've met somebody special?" My response in sheer indignant fashion was, "Do you think that I am THAT shallow to move my daughter across the country for a man?!" I admit I was pretty stupid when it came to relationships but not that stupid to uproot

my entire life and that of my daughter's for a relationship.
That would be a pretty foolish move. Now, if you've done
something like this, I hope that you were truly being led by
the Holy Spirit (and not your flesh), and that it worked out
for you. If it did not work out for you, shake it off, and
keep it movin'. You will never learn how to live right until
you have lived wrong long enough. Plus, you become a
living witness, and I can guarantee you somebody
somewhere right now is relying on your testimony.

Feeling the pressure to be married though does not
necessarily have to come in a direct verbal statement from
someone. It is in the sermons when relational anecdotes
are delivered. Preachers most often reference husbands
and wives and the dynamics and the trials and triumphs of
marriage. Women in the church start getting hitched left
and right, and you turn around and wonder why none of
the single men (the five of them that were there) noticed
you. Rather than sitting beside your soon-to-be-husband,
you are sitting next to Deacon Wilma who is in her sixty's,
has never been married, and has probably never been
kissed! Then, you begin to wonder if you will end up like
Deacon Wilma, and when people ask you if you are dating,
you reply, "Jesus alone; He's all I need!" You know that's a
lie from the pit of hell, but you don't want to sound
desperate, so your reply begins to sound like the foolish
cry from the women of Generation X, "I don't need a
man. I can pay my own bills and raise my own kids." Not
fully understanding the consequences of being a single

parent, and the ramifications that it has both on you and your children.

Another sign of the pressure to be married is when you head home for the holidays, and you gather with your siblings and your extended family. Everyone else has kids and spouses, but you are in the kitchen helping your momma prepare the meal, while pulling double duty preparing activities for your nieces and nephews. But, what you are not doing is fixing your husband a plate or introducing your new boo to the family. Holidays can be hard on single women, even if they do not express it outwardly. As they get older, single women are likely to experience an emptiness or an inward single-fatigue. The older a woman gets the more difficult it becomes to mask the elephant in the room or the elephant *not* in the room—her man! People start to think, "Well, what's wrong with Jackie? How come she can't find a man?" Or, "How come she can't keep a man?" It may never have crossed people's minds that Jackie came from a single-parent household where her momma never had a man or never knew how to be in a successful and fruitful relationship; therefore, Jackie does not know what it is like to be in a relationship because she never witnessed a healthy relationship in her home. Perhaps, Jackie's single mom thought all men were deadbeats and good-for-nothing's, and she lived by the anthem, "I can do bad all by myself!" Jackie could also have come from a two-parent household where her father was too busy and too pre-occupied to notice her and never showed her what true love is, whether intentional or unintentional, so therefore Jackie never knew what to look for in a good man.

The bottom line is **many women are still single because they don't know how to be coupled.** Their expectations are low because they honestly don't know what to expect. They think just because they are cute, have a job, a little bit of intelligence, and know Jesus, that they satisfy the criteria for marriage. Marriage surpasses that standard by far. Loving someone unconditionally and receiving unconditional love is a construct that is out of this world. Being a wife requires an anointing. To devote your life to someone for the rest of your time on earth is supernatural. It is not all fun and games or about the butterflies you feel in your stomach during your first three months of dating. It requires you to shed your earthly realities and constructs of relationships and take on a heavenly mantel that looks everything like Ephesians 5 and I Peter 3. This kind of love and devotion requires you to put yourself last and your husband first.

Single women sometimes feel they are not as significant and valued by both society and the church because they are single. It's almost as if they are a bad omen or a perpetual burden. Sometimes, this feeling is warranted by the way they are treated and looked down on. This is a very difficult conundrum on many levels, but particularly it is very perplexing in the church. Church membership is largely comprised of women. Only <u>two out of every six</u> Christian men attend church regularly[v]. What woman of God wants a man who is not committed to attending church and regularly? When we settle for a man who says he loves God and is a Christian, but he is not devoted to sitting under a man of God where he can grow in the things of God and be discipled and developed by someone with an anointing to teach and shepherd, we are creating an atmosphere where we are unequally yoked. You go to church and receive revelation from the Word, and then come home to a husband who is not receiving that same Word. You are active and involved, are being a blessing and serving the church, whereas your husband is at home, sleeping late and serving himself in front of the television, watching football. Your spiritual walk is not in alignment. How can two walk together, unless they be agreed? (Amos 3:3). One is growing in the faith, the other remaining stagnant. Just imagine how much power and anointing will flood your marriage and what you can do for the kingdom together if you are both on the same page about your spiritual development. When you and your spouse are speaking the same language, there is nothing you can't do. Let me provide you with a biblical example. When God created the earth, He created men to speak the same language. There was only one language on the whole earth. The thousands of languages and dialects that we bear witness to today, were not how God established things in the beginning.

Many women are still single because they don't know how to be coupled.

In Genesis 11, the sons of men came together speaking the same language to build a city and a tower that reached to the heavens—known as the Tower of Babel. When God took notice of the unity and oneness of the people, Genesis 11:6 describes God's reaction to the power of their unity, "If as one people speaking the same language they have begun to do this, then nothing they plan to do will be impossible for them." (New International Version). When you and your husband speak the same language, then NOTHING you plan to do will be impossible for you!! This is why it is critically important for you to marry a man of the faith. But, also, scope out his commitment and devotion to his faith. Make sure there's some consistency there if this is really important to you.

And, let me say this, if giving is important to you, make sure you have a conversation about giving and tithing. Personally, this is a non-negotiable. One Christian man I dated a few times, actually said to me, "I can't afford to tithe." Excuse me, "You can't afford **not** to tithe!" You don't want to bring a curse upon your finances if tithing and giving is what you believe, trust and believe me. You may think that you can change your man's mind after the wedding, but if he does not have revelation now on the importance of tithing, giving, and sowing – only an act of God can change that not your coercion.

Looking back, the many men I dated did not attend church regularly, if at all. One excuse was, "I don't need a man telling me how to live my life. I can talk to God directly." Some men even take it a step further and honestly believe that pastors have a coercive influence over the women in the church and preach messages that make them vulnerable and dependent upon the pastor. The message is, "Pastors are pimps. That's why churches are filled with desperate single women." This could be true in some circumstances, but by and large, this is hogwash and sheer ignorance. Pastors who are truly called by God are called to be shepherds not vultures. They are called and ordained by God to feed the sheep. They are held to a higher standard by the Father, and God does not play with His sheep! When pastors sleep around with the women in the church, embezzle the church funds, and manipulate their membership, they have to answer to God, and you better believe they will.

Woman of God, **recognize that you hold true value just the way you are**. Your man of God will recognize and see the God in you, once you recognize and see the God in yourself. Once you understand that you are validated by being a child of God and nothing more, you will begin to step into your true calling of becoming a wife. Don't allow the pressure of marriage to weigh you down. And don't question whether God has called you to marriage. Woman was created out of man because God felt that Adam needed a helper. He created you to be suitable and complimentary to a man, to your husband.

God created you for earthly companionship. The Word of God says two are better than one in Ecclesiastes 4:9-12.

Finally, God won't give His children desires He does not intend to fulfill. If you are reading this book, almost unequivocally, you have a strong desire to be married. Your loving, gracious, and merciful Father intends to fulfill that desire. But, before you tie the knot, make sure you have done more than just planned for a wedding. Many men and women spend so much time planning a wedding, they forget to plan for their MARRIAGE! When you fail to plan your marriage, you end up a statistic. Between forty and fifty percent of all first-time marriages end in divorce[vi]. No one intends for their marriage to end in divorce, but without the proper cultivation and due diligence ahead of time, in many cases divorce is inevitable. Of course, God is merciful and can rescue your marriage from divorce, but why jeopardize your marriage in the first place by neglecting the proper courtship?

It is in your BEST interest to thoroughly vet your future spouse. We spend more time researching home purchases and graduate schools than we do researching a prospective mate and investing in pre-marital counseling. If you would invest in a four-year college degree by forking over thousands of dollars, why would you neglect to spend three-to-four meager weeks in pre-marriage counseling that costs as low as $200, and in many cases is freely provided at your local church? Does that make ANY

KIND OF SENSE? Do not rush the process. What God has for you is for you. Time cannot delay God's promises for your life. Divorce is the enemy's most reliable confidant—it wreaks havoc on families and does the greatest damage to future generations. We must stop divorce in its tracks by completely relying on the Holy Spirit to do His work in you and your future mate before you make any decisions that are binding. It's been said many times, getting married is easy—staying married is the true work.

MAJOR THEMES

- Don't get tired of holding out when a man asks you to put out. The reward will be greater than the temporary pleasure.
- Your happiness and your worth as a woman should not be based on your relationship status.
- Every time you compromise your standards, you reduce the full value of what you have to offer in a relationship.
- Pay close attention to red flags in relationships. Don't ignore the obvious.
- Just because he goes to church, doesn't mean he should have an automatic pass to your heart.
- Many women find themselves single long-term because they don't know how to be coupled.

ELEVATION

Why do you want to be married? It's important to fully understand your desire for marriage so that you can posture yourself for marriage God's way. Some people get married because they believe two incomes are better than one income. Others because they are in love with the idea of marriage but aren't ready or willing to do the necessary work. There are myriad reasons why people tie the knot. Why do you want to get married? Write your most authentic response in the accompanying notebook or in your private journal. Don't write what you think is the "right" response, write what you truly believe at this stage of your life. After you've written your response, see if your response aligns with God's desire for marriage.

Part III: Avoid Toxic Relationships

"If you are unclear about what your desires are, you will get anything, and you will settle for everything."

As women, most of us have a picture in our heads of what our dream man looks like. For some, he's basketball-player tall, dark-skinned, lean, with a nice fade, and a stroll. For others, he is light-skinned, average height, nice build—like he is getting good miles out of his gym membership—with wavy hair—the kind that when you run your fingers through it, your fingers get basted with grease! My point is, most women have an image of their ideal man in their head. I will go even further and say that many of us have an image of our ideal husband. The kind of man that we want to build a life with and have children with. We spend hours fantasizing about the totality that makes up this man. Then when we start dating and eventually find ourselves in a relationship, we begin to fantasize even more. I'm sure I'm not the first woman, who when dating someone I really liked, wrote my first name and his last name to see if there was a "ring" to the way the names sounded together. No matter how crazy the names sounded together, you are convinced that if this thing works out, that is the best name combo ever!

And, why do we as women plan a wedding after our first date? I've been guilty of this myself. Every time we start to get serious feelings for a man, we begin to look at our calendar to see when the ideal time for a wedding is, check with our HR department to see how many vacation days we have accrued, check the sorority calendar to ensure there are no major events planned around that time, begin drafting a list of our potential bridesmaids, and check the savings account to see if there is any money available to contribute toward the wedding expenses. You done planned an entire wedding, and the man barely even said that he liked you! Pump your breaks!

Have you taken the time to verify this man's credentials? What are his beliefs? Does he have an unabashed spiritual core? Is that even important to you? What are his short and long-term goals? How does he manage his finances? Does he have any finances to manage? Does he maintain steady work, or does he change jobs like you change your weave? What is his relationship with his family? How does he treat his mother? Does he have children? How does he treat his baby's mother? Is he dating other women? Does he have a girlfriend? Does he have a wife? Let me ask that again, **does he have a wife?** If he used to be married, is he legally divorced? Have you seen the divorce decree? Does he have a criminal record? Is he a swinger? Does he have a terminal disease/illness? Is he on the down-low? Is he gay? Does he attend church? If so, does he attend regularly? Is he a tither? If so, is he a consistent tither? You get my drift, no need to belabor, but can you answer these questions for yourself? Do these questions matter to you based on your values? Until you can answer these questions (and others) with certainty, you need to have several seats and temper your emotions until you receive clarity and guidance from the Lord.

Most women don't sit down when they are daydreaming about their future husband and say, "I want to be in a relationship with a much older man with a family of his own that just takes care of me financially." And what woman do you know who has said, "My ideal man is one who is already messing around with another woman, since there don't appear to be options elsewhere." And have you ever heard a woman say, "I want to fall in love with a married man so that I can be his mistress, live in hiding for five years, and reap absolutely no benefit other than occasional good sex." Although I never endeavored to experience any of these scenarios, I have lived them, and many women are living them every day because they do not recognize their value and their status as queens in the earth.

When you come to the end of the heartbreak, the agony, the selfishness, and the delusion; when you come to the end of yourself, you will begin to recognize that your worth is simply in being a child of God. Period. You don't need to do anything else to prove you are worthy of love, honor, respect, and devotion. You don't need to sleep around. You don't need to be the center of attention. You don't need to be jealous. You don't need to try to take someone else's man. You don't need to try and get a man to impregnate you just to keep him. You don't need to do any of that. YOU ARE WORTHY OF REAL LOVE.

Just to be clear, most women don't find themselves in a state of ignorance and delusion by happenstance or of their own volition. Men have an important role to play. God created man to be a covering for his woman—to honor her and to protect her heart. Many men (and women) do not understand the importance of protecting a woman's heart, and so we often end up with two incomplete and confused people coming together in a relationship to multiply their confusion until it becomes a hot mess! But, because God placed man in a position of leadership the moment he created him out of the dust of the ground, He assigned to man a higher level of accountability.

This chapter focuses on an imbalance of that accountability and a dearth of leadership and proper perspective on relationships. We'll talk about some common toxic relationships that keep you bound and your life stagnant. Specifically, I talk about the sugar daddy relationship, the three-way-relationship (being in a relationship with an unmarried man who is in a relationship with one or several other women), and the married man. These are real every day issues that we need to be talking about more, openly. I end the chapter with additional insight on the purpose of a man's position in every relationship, and God's original intent for man.

Avoid the Sugar Daddy

A sugar daddy is defined as, "a wealthy middle-aged man who spends freely on a young woman in return for her companionship or intimacy.[vii]" Awh...the infamous Sugar Daddy, or what I like to call, "Hugh Hefner Syndrome". An older man who sees a young woman as impressionable and sweeps her off her feet with lavish gifts in exchange for companionship and the thrill of having a young beauty on his arm. I met my sugar daddy at my campus job during undergrad. The funny thing is, he was neither wealthy nor middle-aged. He was actually past the middle and balding! He was a nice man that showed concern for me, and so initially, I just considered him to be a friend.

He was probably old enough to be my grandfather, so I was too naive to think that this man had any kind of feelings for me. It became more apparent as he started offering to pay my phone bill and began buying me groceries, that he probably looked at me as more than just a young lady who he was helping out of the kindness of his heart. As our relationship grew, he invited me to travel with him on a business trip—all expenses paid. It was then that it became painfully obvious to me that this man wanted more than my friendship, especially when I discovered that he only paid for one hotel room with one king-sized bed. I thought to myself, "Where you sleepin, bruh?!"

I was only twenty-three-years-old at the time and was still young and dumb. Thankfully, this man never approached me in a romantic manner, and I only credit that to God's covering on my life. But, there are plenty of women that have willingly flaunted their sugar daddies in public, along with the enticing perks that come with the relationship—from designer handbags, to new cars, to trips, and cash. The glamour of being treated like a queen and having nice things all in exchange for companionship is an even exchange to some women.

But, this is not reality, and certainly not what God intended for relationships. And, in many cases, these men are married with children, unbeknownst to the woman. If you are in a relationship with a sugar daddy, it is likely because you did not have a strong relationship with your own daddy growing up, and so, you are not only finding provision in this relationship, but you are also finding fatherhood. You may feel like you are getting your needs met, but the relationship is imbalanced and unsustainable for two reasons. One, once the man you are spending time with and giving sexual favors to (in some cases) becomes bored with you, discovers you do not live up to his expectations, and finds someone new to spoil—there goes your provision. Two, no man on earth can possibly meet your every need—the only One qualified to do that is God. Whenever you place your complete hope and expectation in a man—you WILL BE DISAPPOINTED every single time. Men are imperfect beings, so why would you put the full weight of your life on another imperfect being?

Three's a Crowd

As I mentioned before, I attended an historically Black university for my undergraduate degree. The excitement I felt about attending an all-Black school was through the roof! Particularly, because I grew up in predominantly White communities most of my childhood. When I first discovered there were large proportions of young and educated Black people in one location—it was almost unbelievable! I was in heaven. I was quickly introduced, however, to the reality of the gender divide at HBCU's (Historical Black Colleges and Universities) and most college campuses. The male-to-female ratio at these schools is on average, <u>one male to every two-and-half females</u>[viii]. Which essentially means that during the formative and carefree years of college, Black men have the pick of the litter on Black college campuses, while Black women are left clamoring for whatever is available or sharing what is there. Granted, college is not a place where your first ambition should be to pursue or be pursued. But, we all know that college is one big social experiment, where for many young teens and twenty-somethings, it is their first experience with independence and their first opportunity to identify with themselves and with a larger community of hormones that are raging about in study halls, college dorms, and fraternity and sorority parties.

What many young girls enter college thinking is, they will meet the man of their dreams or at least meet a prospective man who is available and at minimum, agrees to monogamy. Many young girls, however, discover the exact opposite. They meet a cute boy who they think has eyes only for them, give up the cookie, and then months later, find out some other girl is also serving up dessert in a dorm on the other end of campus or in some cases in the same dormitory! One would think upon discovery and reflection, that one of the women or both, would kick said trifle to the curb. But, nope! They cop an initial attitude with the dessert thief, give the other girl the side-eye, but continue in the relationship.

This pattern of "man-sharing" continues into adulthood. Even, if you are one to believe you are a one-woman man and that you would never ever share your man with another woman, never say never. There are many women who shared this sentiment initially and ended up settling because they believed that *a* man was better than *no* man. And, let's be honest, most women do not purposely seek out a man who is already in a relationship with another woman. What woman in her right mind wants to share a man? Notice I said, "What woman in her **right** mind?" There are women that are into this whole concept of "swinging," or who are vindictive and straight up triflin', and will pursue a man relentlessly while he is in a relationship with another woman. These women do exist. But, by and large, most women who find themselves in a three-way relationship, find out about the other woman after the fact, and just find the task of letting go too difficult or inconvenient on their flesh. That certainly was the case with me.

About a year and a half after I graduated from college, I decided I did not want to work in the profession for which I had pursued my degree, so I took a job that would pay me quick money, until I discovered what I really wanted to do. On my new job, I ran into a man who started to pique my interest, named Derrick. Derrick was a bit corny, and I really thought he was a weird valley-boy initially, but the more I got to know him and talk to him, I discovered there was actual intellect underneath that dorky facade of his. Intellect has always been the thing that hooks me—looks are a close second, but if you can stimulate my mind, you have effectively stimulated me.

Derrick and I started hanging out after work and eventually word got back to me that he was dating another girl at our job, named Amanda. I confronted him about it, and he told me that he and Amanda were together at one point but had broken up. Well, unbeknown to me, that wasn't entirely true. He and I continued to see each other. Throughout the time we were seeing each other, Amanda would give me the evil eye whenever we shared shifts at work. "Why is she hating because her ex likes me?" I thought to myself. Truthfully, I had no alliance to Amanda. I knew Derrick before I ever met her, so I figured she had no reason to be mad at me for being next in line.

Eventually, I discovered not only was Derrick still in a relationship with Amanda, but he was also in a relationship with his daughter's mother. I'm talking actual relationships, where he has both women believing he is solely committed to each of them. What kind of shenanigans?! This man, as it turns out, had a problem with serial dating and serial lying. He would look you dead in the face and tell you, you were his only one, then have several relationships happening all at once—and juggled it masterfully! Really, it seems like too much to have on one's conscience, but he didn't appear stressed at all. After, I discovered I was in the middle of a love triangle—

or a love quadrangle? I was foolish enough to allow this man to continue to be in an intimate relationship with me, until I finally came to myself weeks later.

Like this PITIFUL example demonstrates, many women do not believe they deserve better, and so they settle for whatever bone is thrown their way. I know women who have been in relationships with men for YEARS, and yet they still do not have any real commitment and are too afraid to ask the man if he is seeing other women. Some of these women have full knowledge they are not the only person involved with the man and have simply settled. The Word of God says to take delight in the Lord, and He will give you the desires of your heart (Psalm 37:4). **If you are unclear about what your desires are, you will get anything, and you will settle for everything.** Do you really desire to be in a relationship with a man who cannot commit himself to you and only you? Is that the kind of man you want to build a life with?

Run Like Hell from a Married Man

This section could have been a book all its own. The subtitle may sound a bit exaggerated, but it isn't. Run like hell if a married man gives even the slightest hint that he is interested in you. If you do not run like hell, hell will come running after you.

If you are unclear about what your desires are, you will get anything, and you will settle for everything.

I don't care if the man tells you he is separated and has been separated for months or for years, that he is awaiting his divorce decree, or that he and his wife are estranged. If the man is married—FLEE! I have lost track of the number of married men that have come on to me at some point during my season of singleness—both inside and outside of the church. Let me say that again, both inside and outside of the church!

Because this issue is so prominent and is very non-discriminatory, I am compelled to speak out about it in the hopes that women would come to grips with who the Creator of the world purposed them to be—wives not mistresses. I learned this the hard way after being in a relationship with a married man for five years. You read that correctly. Let me first say, in no way am I proud of the decision I made to engage in an extramarital affair, just like I am not proud of many of the decisions I made in my former life. It was God's mercy that delivered me and His grace that enabled me to walk away. I now know God was preparing me to share my story with other women who too have found themselves either in the midst of or pondering intimacy with a married man. It happens more than we'd like to admit, and I'm confident either you or someone close to you, can relate to this experience. There are countless women who share my story. Many without the strength to walk away. You may find yourself hoping and even praying that the man you fell for would leave his wife one day. Like me, you may have absorbed, meditated on, and believed every loving word this married man uttered about how much he loves you and desires to be in a committed relationship with you.

Our stories and the stories of many other women around the globe, are the same. We don't really understand how foolish and naive the very concept of a man leaving his wife for a mistress is until years later—once we have had an opportunity to step back and look at our mess and the damage we have caused and ask ourselves, "What in the hell was I thinking?!" If you cannot relate to what I am talking about in this section, DON'T SKIP THIS OVER. Read it in its entirety because if you are a woman who is not spending time with the Lord and in His Word, this could VERY easily happen to you. Also, what you learn here could be a blessing to someone you know.

I am revealing my naked truth so that you or someone you know can be free. If you find yourself in these pages as you read this section, my desire for you is that you finally open your eyes and see how your soul is being incrementally severed. It won't hit you right away, but it happens in stages. A lie here, a promise there, until your emotions are completely stripped. Eventually, you will be convinced about the lie you are living, and your entire rationale will change, just so that you can justify remaining in a relationship that will only leave you hurting in the end, and the man that you 'love' staying right where he is—in his marriage. Let me tell you, liberation feels so good!

And, I am confident that you, too will be liberated, so the door can be open for you to receive the man God has truly prepared for you who is simply waiting on you to leave your past and that triflin' married man behind.

The Sheltering Backfire

I grew up in a sheltered environment. Being the only daughter of an ordained minister, I was not allowed to have boyfriends, hang out late after school, listen to most secular music, or watch any movies that had even the slightest hint of sexually explicit undertones. My parents had a tight rein on me. Being the only girl among three brothers didn't help. Some people say preacher's kids are the worst kind. Well, I wasn't the worst, but I'm sure I was in second place. As a teenager, I did anything and everything I could to gain attention. I shoplifted, ran away, lied routinely, and went on secret rendezvous, you name it. All in the name of the desire to be wanted, valued, noticed, and validated. It is amazing and unfortunate how I hear parents or parents-to-be say they aren't going to let their daughters date until they are off in college or off on their own somewhere. Some may be saying that in jest, yet many have no idea how detrimental freedom restriction can be to their daughter's development and ability to successfully and mindfully select worthwhile companions and eventually a husband. Being overly sheltered and not having the opportunity to experience the complexities of relationships, being denied the opportunity to experience a man's attention, or lacking the dating experience necessary to be successful at dating as an adult, leads too many women into physically, verbally, sexually, and emotionally abusive relationships.

My upbringing, coupled with the rebellious nature which ensued, led me to become extremely naive and vulnerable to any form of influence as an inexperienced and impressionable young woman looking for validation. By the time I fell into the relationship that I discuss in this section, I thought I had learned everything I needed to know and experienced all of the heartache necessary to fully make myself available for a genuine and mutually exclusive relationship. It turns out I had much more growing up to do. When I entered this extramarital relationship, I entered into a spiritual realm where I never imagined I would be. A place where I desperately wanted in and wanted out, all at the same time. In the chambers of my heart, I knew the relationship was destined to fail. But, my every thought and every action was controlled and influenced by false hope. The hope of being loved, desired, esteemed, honored, protected, and nurtured by someone incapable of providing me with these things. I believed this man was everything that I ever wanted and needed. I was in a six-foot pit of delusion. I had dug my own grave without even noticing the shovel in my hand.

The Ultimate Downfall
We met because we had mutual interests—serving the needs of the African-American community. He was a

medical doctor at a local hospital, and I was fresh out of undergrad, starting out on a noteworthy business venture—helping students of color prepare their portfolios for college.

I vividly recollect our first introduction. We were both volunteers on an inaugural community service project. At our first planning meeting, he was introduced as a surgeon and a scholar—Dr. Michael Cofield. The moment I heard him speak, I was smitten. He didn't mince his words. He spoke with intention, intelligence, insight, and passion. I was mesmerized by his aura, and like any sensible single woman, I was hoping and praying he wasn't married.

So, I made it a point after the meeting to position myself next to this Dr. Cofield for an introduction. "Hi, I'm Michael Cofield," he said. I was encouraged that he did not introduce himself to me as "Dr. Cofield" as to intimidate me. His body language and eye contact were fixated on me. My speech was not impressive, and yet he seemed to be hanging on to my every word. I made light of it because I didn't want to make any assumptions. We exchanged business cards and planned a follow-up meeting at his office—just the two of us.

A week goes by, and I'm sitting in Dr. Cofield's office discussing business. Somehow, during our meeting, the tone of our discourse changed from business to personal. Michael began to share with me that he was separated from his wife, at which point sent my mind racing. I convinced myself I was there for business and nothing more. But, in reality, my body language was signaling something different. I came into his office with my soul wide-open and my pores giving off an aroma of vulnerability. The attraction I had for him far outweighed my professional disposition. The moment he told me he was separated, I felt free to let down my guard, and I immediately felt a spiritual, emotional, and physical tie to him. I became so vulnerable in that moment and was scared to death because I could not understand why I barely knew this man, just discovered the inconvenient truth that he was married, but instantly felt like I could not live without him. I felt as if I were both drowning and floating in one emotion.

I fought Michael off for a whole year. Repeatedly, I would remind myself that he was not legally divorced, and I had no business being with a married man. I tried avoiding him at all costs, but his pursuit was relentless. His voice became something I anxiously anticipated and eventually agonized over being without. As the first year ended, I simply could not fight his advances any more. I desperately felt like I needed to seal physically what had already been birthed spiritually. And, so, I found myself, at the age of twenty-five, making love to a married man. In our moment of passion, I immediately knew I had just unlocked the door to the demise of my soul.

The next four years were a blur. I was the ultimate pretender. Nobody ever knew. I was singing on the worship team on Sunday morning and sleeping with a married man on Sunday night. I lived at the intersection of delusion and depression. I became convinced that "my" man would leave his wife and begin a life with me. And, because our relationship was as tempestuous as it was tumultuous, I kept kicking him to the curb and taking him right back. Every time I tried fighting him off, I wanted him back even more. Even after I discovered he was still spending time with his family, I still could not break free. He became my addiction.

Five years had come and gone, and there I was—still hoping, still longing, still waiting, still addicted to a married man. Toward the end of year five, on the umpteenth time that I "broke up with him," I met someone who I thought was Michael's replacement. I said to myself, "Certainly this man must be my husband!" It turned out that this new man was also legally married, although he and his wife were noticeably separated, and they were actively working through their divorce. Still, I should've known better! At this point, I had gone from delusional to delirious! Because this was another recipe for disaster, God only allowed the relationship to last for a few months. But, in that time, I was completely released from the desire for Michael. Now, I can admit, it was not a wise move to go from one disastrous relationship to another with hopes that this new relationship could mend my brokenness and possibly lead to a more hopeful outcome. However, in God's infinite grace, it was His way of rescuing me and saving me further humiliation and despair, since I lacked the power to break free from him on my own. Thank God He pitied me enough to intervene—even in a most unconventional way.

It took several years for me to completely heal from my relationship with Michael, but early on in that healing process, I came across this passage in my daily devotional:

> God will often extricate us from the mess we have made, because 'his love endures forever' (I Chronicles 16:34). Yet if we had only been patient and waited to see the unfolding of His plan, we would never have found ourselves in such an impossible maze, seeing no way out. We would also never have had to turn back and retrace our way, with wasted steps and so many tears of shame.[ix]

There is nothing tantalizing about being in an affair. I don't care about the thrill that you think comes with it, believe me when I say any thrill that you feel is short-lived. Being the other woman destroys your soul. Most at issue though, is the fact you are contributing to the demise of a family. **If a man tells you he is separated, he is still in a covenant relationship—one that God has consecrated and ordained.** Unless that covenant becomes legally severed, you have no rights to the property of another woman. And, if you think the man will eventually marry you, data show that second and third marriages are more likely to fail than first-time marriages. So, if you were to marry this man, the chances of your marriage surviving are slim, at best.

Keep your hands off a married man. Keep your mind off him and protect your soul from being tied to his. If you already find yourself in an affair, and you feel like it is impossible to get out; there is a way out. Get on your knees and pour your heart out to God. God is a God of mercy. He will forgive you, wipe your slate clean, and give you a second chance. Ask God to replace your desires for this man with desires for Him. Fill your life with things that edify and activities which are aligned with your life's purpose. The only good that can come from your relationship with a married man is your testimony. Now, that you have a testimony, get out, immediately.

The Abdication

One thing that is not discussed as often as it should be—is the very important role of the man in relationships and his natural position of authority. I would posit that many relationship woes could be avoided entirely when a man and woman enter a marriage with the understanding of their respective positions in the marital union. When God created humanity and everything that we can see and everything that we cannot see with our natural eyes, he created man to lead it. It's Bible. Let me explain.

If a man tells you he is separated, he is still in a covenant relationship—one that God has consecrated and ordained.

Several thousand years ago in the Garden of Eden, sin entered the world. Many of us are familiar with "The Fall of Man" in Genesis 3, but I want to walk you through the passage and shed some new light on the story in a way you may not have considered before.

In Genesis 3:2, Eve tells the snake that although they can eat fruit from the trees in the Garden, God commanded them not to eat the fruit from the tree in the middle of the Garden, and if they did, they would die. The snake then lies to Eve in verse 4 and tells her she will not die, but that instead, she will learn about good and evil. This piques Eve's interest. Verse 6 is where the world gets turned upside down:

> "The woman could see that the tree was beautiful, and the fruit looked so good to eat. She also liked the idea that it would make her wise. So, she took some of the fruit from the tree and ate it. **Her husband was there with her, so she gave him some of the fruit, and he ate it.**" (New International Version).

Adam makes two mistakes in this passage. First, he allows the enemy to continue to tempt and entice his wife to do something that God gave Adam clear instructions NOT to do. God told Adam, prior to Eve's formation, not to eat from the tree of the knowledge of good and evil:

> "And the Lord God commanded the man, 'You are free to eat from any tree in the garden; but you must not eat from

the tree of the knowledge of good and evil, for when you eat from it you will certainly die." Genesis 2:16-17 (New International Version)

Right after this passage, in verse 18, God creates Eve, which would suggest that Eve received instructions not to eat from the tree from her husband, Adam.

Adam's second mistake is that he allows his wife to commit a sin right in front of him, and then participates in the sin himself. Rather than Adam taking his position as a leader, he gets out of position and allows his wife to be tempted, and they both fall deep into sin—fundamentally altering the course of the world and changing God's original intent for man.

Even more, Adam abdicates himself from the sin, assigning the blame to his wife, his queen, Eve—the First Lady of Humanity. God intended husbands to stand in front of their wives, to provide cover. Rather than taking blame for the sin as Eve's covering, Adam punts:

"The man said, 'The woman you put here with me—she gave me some fruit from the tree, and I ate it.' Genesis 3:12 (New International Version)

Hence, *The Abdication.* Unfortunately, what happened in the Garden of Eden thousands of years ago, continues today, and the impact has been significant. Oftentimes, instead of providing shelter for their women and fully owning their leadership role, many men have relaxed and retreated. There is no shortage of scenarios to illustrate this point. You can look at the scores of families that show up for church on Sunday without the father/husband present. You can look at the single parent households where many men decide, for one reason or another, they don't want to be fathers. You can look at the marriages that remain stagnant for years, where the husband is emotionally and oftentimes spiritually or even financially inept.

This is not an attempt to bash men nor to put all the responsibility on them. Wives and women in general play their part in producing marriage and relationship woes. Many wives have not received revelation on how to be a wife, which too, is problematic. This leads them to step way out of position—which is what Eve did in the Garden. Then, there are single mothers who are manipulative and use their children as weapons in relationships. These actions are both ignorant and detrimental. My point is, like a pastor is the shepherd of his flock—the parishioners of the church, the husband is called to be the shepherd of his home—casting vision and leading by example. In the same vein, women should be mindful of the influence they bring to the relationship/marriage and walk in that role accordingly, just the same. Unfortunately, since many men and women were not raised to understand positioning in marriage, these issues perpetuate.

God's intentions for families was that one man would marry one woman and that the man would be the spiritual head of the household, while the wife would be the man's capable and competent helper. In no way weaker, or subservient to the man but to complement him with her unique talents and strengths. This was God's original intent for humanity. Men and women must understand their original design and walk in it. With men walking in their place as leaders and women walking alongside them—infidelity, divorce, and broken hearts and homes will be a thing of the past.

So, my sister, your heart should be for a man who understands his role and lives according to the knowledge of his position in the earth. If you do not have clarity about how a man should lead, take a seat, and get some understanding. Do not look for companionship until you receive absolute revelation on God's original intent for marriage. It's right there in the Word.

And, know your role and your worth, honey. You are worth more than a man fantasizing over your body and idolizing your beauty, just so he can buy you a designer hand bag and carry you on his arm. You are worth more than splitting your time and sharing your body with a man who is not in a covenant relationship with you and is spreading his sperm all around town—going from one woman's bed to the next. Don't you think you deserve your own man? One who respects you enough to value just you? Trust me; you do. Just be patient.

And, you most certainly are worth more than sleeping with a married man. A man who is married and decides to cheat on his wife with you, is not considering your needs—he is only considering his own. And, no matter how much he says he loves you, you and he are both delusional if you believe what you have is love. Love is self-less, not selfish. What you both are displaying is selfishness. Love is sacrificial—it is the act of giving up something for the good of someone else. If you are in a relationship with a man who is not giving up something for the betterment of your life, it's time to close the door on that chapter and move on to the next.

MAJOR THEMES

- You are worthy of real love.
- If you are unclear about what your desires are, you will get anything, and you will settle for everything.
- Run LIKE HELL from a married man. Run, don't walk!
- Do not look for a father in your relationship in an attempt to fill the void of not having your own physically active father.
- No man on earth can meet your every need. Only God can do that.

- God placed man in first position to lead as the head of the household.

ELEVATION

Good **single** men do exist. They are not a figment of your imagination. Happily, ever after can happen for you if you believe it, and if you prepare your life to receive it. Do you know what kind of marriage you want? What qualities does God want you to consider for your future husband? If you haven't prayed about these things, anything and anyone is bound to come your way. Take the time now to write out a description of the kind of marriage God desires for you, and the qualities you desire in your husband.

Part IV: Return to Your First Love

"But he was wounded for our transgressions, he was bruised for our iniquities: the chastisement of our peace was upon him; and with his stripes we are healed." Isaiah 53:5
(King James Version).

"No one has greater love [no one has shown stronger affection] than to lay down (give up) his own life for his friends." John 15:13 (Amplified Bible, Classic Edition)

The greatest love story of all time is found on the cross. Let me repeat that: **the greatest love story in history is found on the cross at Calvary** where the Savior of the World chose to lay his life down for you and me. To be able to comprehend the full understanding of LOVE, one need look no further than the cross. The cross is the only reason why you and I have hope.

Imagine for a moment, what life would be like if Isaiah 53:5 were never fulfilled? If in His darkest hour, when

Jesus cried out to God, "Father, if you are willing, take this cup from me; yet not my will, but yours be done," He changes His mind about going to the cross? Even though Jesus' soul was sorely vexed, he persevered because in that moment He saw an image of you fulfilling your assignment in the earth. He also saw an image of your children, their children, and several generations throughout the course of time, and He knew His obedience had implications beyond Himself—the entire world was hinging on His obedience.

Imagine the weight of the responsibility that Jesus carried. He literally carried the weight of the world on His shoulders. But, so do you and I. In Romans 8:19 it says, "For the creation waits in eager expectation for the children of God to be revealed." (New International Version). You can't be revealed if you are still stuck in damaging and depleting relationships; if you are still waiting on a ring, or waiting on him to leave his wife, or waiting on him to change his ways. The longer you wait, the longer your gifts and talents and true potential are being stifled and suffocated. It's reminiscent of a caged bird. Birds and other reptiles and mammals aren't meant to be caged. They were created to roam about the earth to explore, to live, and to fulfill their purpose. When they are left in a cage, they eventually lose their vitality, and their lifespan is shortened. That's what happens when we allow things that do not align with God's will to consume our lives. We end up losing our vitality, and we die an early death without having truly fulfilled our assignment in the earth. Do you want that to be your story—over a relationship?!

Jesus was the ultimate example of living a purpose-driven life. He was driven solely and exclusively by his destiny—not by people, relationships, or things that are all brief and fleeting but by purpose which is found in the Father.

"Looking unto Jesus the author and finisher of our faith; who for the joy that was set before him endured the cross, despising the shame, and is set down at the right hand of the throne of God." Hebrews 12:2 (King James Version)

Jesus considered it pure joy to lay His life down for you. With that in mind, it shouldn't take an act of God to get you to lay your life down for Him in return. **Many women are quick to lay their body down for a man but slow to lay their life down for Christ**. Christ was there in the very beginning. He will outlive every one-night-stand, relationship, and *NetFlix and Chill*[1] situation you will ever encounter.

It is time to return to your First Love. His Name is Jesus—the Name Above ALL names. He is your defender, your advocate, your helper, and your intercessor. He has been and continues to be the one constant that will

---

[1] Blame this terminology on the Millennials. Visit www.urbandictionary.com to learn the meaning.

never give up on you and will not stop pursuing you. When you are in your darkest moments, God is there. When you are at your wit's end, He is there. When you have repeatedly refused to ignore His promptings and obey His directive, He is still there. Because He loves you without prerequisites and with all your imperfections. Where sin abounds, grace abounds more (Romans 5:20). God has demonstrated His love for you time and time again. It is time for you to recognize and accept His love—knowing His plans for you are good and not evil (Jeremiah 29:11). He intends to fulfill every promise and deliver on every dream. Just return to Him and let Him be everything you need.

> If you are not a believer and have never accepted Jesus Christ into your heart, now is the time to let Him in. God created you and called you into relationship with Him. Go to the Prayer of Salvation in the back of the book, read it, and confess it out loud. You'll be glad you did. If you are a Christian, and you want to live differently, it's time to rededicate your life to Christ. God will always receive you with open arms. Refer to the Prayer of Rededication in the back of the book and confess your prayer to God.

Many women are quick to lay their body down for a man but slow to lay their life down for Christ.

There is a Way of Escape

God is such a merciful God. It doesn't matter what you may have done in your past, God stands at the ready to give you a new heart, change your direction, and love you back into His presence. Sometimes it takes us a while to get to the place of repentance, where we are ready to give up our old life and take on a new life in Him. So, we go from tragedy to tragedy, from confusion to confusion, from bed to bed, and from broken heart to broken heart; wondering internally, when will things ever change? When will I finally have a man of my own who loves me for me and wants nothing from me but my love in return? No casual sex, no lies, no games, no false pretenses and expectations—just love.

When you live according to your flesh, your desires do not align with God's desires. No matter how much you may want something, God has something in mind for you that is far greater than you could ever imagine. However, when you don't wait for the fruit to ripen, and eat the banana while it's still green, the fullness of what God has for you won't be realized, and you will suffer disappointment. BUT, because God is merciful, He will often extricate you from your own mess because you lack the power to do it yourself. I envision God peering over the balcony of heaven, shaking His head at all the times we refuse to allow His best for us. God's thoughts are, "If she only knew what I have for her, she wouldn't bother wasting her time, energy, and emotions on this man. If she could just be patient and refuse to compromise, I would give her beyond her wildest dreams."

I am confident God has said this about me and often. Especially, when I was fresh out of high school and FINALLY had the opportunity to live away from my parents. I had no clue about life or love. My spirit was open to any and everything. After months of being single, I found myself in a relationship with a man who I thought was "making it." He was a successful young entrepreneur and was making very good money for your average twenty-year-old. He had a nice whip, always had money, dressed well, and he liked to spend his money on me. A recipe for success, right?! Wrong. We dated off and on for about four years, though he never wanted an official commitment. All he really wanted from me was occasional companionship and available sex. Since, I didn't know the first thing about love, I obliged him though I really wanted more. Those four years were disastrous. There were discoveries of him being with other women, my personal and financial information being compromised, and then experiencing a dark side of him that reason could not penetrate.

Eventually, our romantic relationship came to an end. I soon became his sounding board and would sit and listen to him talk for hours about his drama with the other women in his life. One day, he called me with fresh excitement about a new woman that he met. He thought

she was gorgeous, and so he intentionally pursued her.
After dating for about a three years, they married. After
the marriage, he and I eventually lost communication, but
when I learned through common connections that there
were reports of domestic violence, until one day someone
called to tell me that his wife of nine years had died at the
tender age of forty.

Immediately, I began to think to myself, "What if this
would've been me?" As much as I wanted to be in a
relationship with this man and would've done anything to
keep him, I could've ended up in an abusive relationship
and possibly lost my life. The moral of the story is, you
never know what God is saving you from. You may want
to be in a relationship with a man so badly that you are
willing to risk your friendships, your dreams, and your
own identity, but are you willing to risk your life? I don't
think you want a man that badly.

I wrote this book to remind you of who you are and what
is available to you. So, rather than remaining in your pit of
delusion or ever falling into the pit at all, you would learn
from the mistakes of those before you and choose to go in
another direction. Let me be your example not to give
your life completely over into the hands of a hu-*man* who
is not capable of loving you the way your heavenly Father
is capable of loving you. No man could ever achieve the
measure of sacrifice that God achieved when He sent His
only son into the world as an exchange for your life. Unless

the man you are with is willing to go to the cross for you by dying to himself and demonstrating his love for you not just in word but in deed also, then you need to bid him farewell and get before God, so you can develop into the woman you were created to be. So, real love can finally be released to come find you.

God Sees You

Many women grow up not fully recognizing their value. They don't believe anyone cares for them and often look for validation through the wrong means. Women wear short and tight clothes, flaunt their bodies, give sexual favors, and put themselves in precarious situations because they think this is the only way to get a man's attention. I've been there. But, living like this is not living at all—it is barely surviving. When you live like this, you experience a constant cycle of manipulation, abuse, isolation, shame, hurt, and fear. You will not obtain the desired result, which is unconditional love, because you don't recognize that all the value and recognition you need is in God.

Genesis 16 shares the story of Hagar. Hagar was an Egyptian slave to Sarah—the wife of Abraham—the father of many nations. God made a promise to Abraham, telling him his offspring would be as numerous as the stars in the sky. The stars in the sky were far too many to count, and that was God's point. Abraham could not possibly count the number of offspring which would come from his bloodline. But, there was one problem. Abraham was long in the tooth (old!) and his wife Sarah had not borne him any children.

Many of you know the story. Sarah comes up with the bright idea to give her slave girl, Hagar to Abraham to fulfill the promise of God. One thing we need to understand is that God DOES NOT need our help to fulfill HIS promises for our lives! If He said it, He will perform it (Numbers 23:19). Stop trying to help God honor His Word by forcing a square peg into a round hole.

Essentially, Sarah forces Hagar to sleep with Abraham, and Hagar gives birth to Ishmael—Abraham's first son. Hagar starts bragging about the fact that she bore Abraham a son and Sarah did not, which results in Sarah treating Hagar harshly and her running away. While Hagar was on the run, she encountered an angel who told her many people would come from her lineage. The Lord recognized the rejection Hagar felt, and Hagar responded in a way that many women respond when they finally acknowledge and receive God's love after experiencing the pain of rejection:

"You are 'God Who Sees Me.'" She said this because she thought, "I see that even in this place God sees me and cares for me!" Genesis 16:13 (Easy-to-Read Version).

There are many women who can identify with Hagar's story. They experience rejection after rejection. They find themselves in relationships with the wrong men, with married men, with men who are already in relationships, and with men who simply do not recognize or value their worth. All the while, God recognizes them. He sees them, and He is simply waiting on them to acknowledge and receive His love.

Know that whatever you are experiencing in life, whatever trial you might be facing, whatever hurtful relationship you might be in—GOD SEES YOU, He loves you, and He considers you worthy of unconditional love. Do yourself a favor and recognize how much God loves you, how valuable you are as His daughter, and go about pursuing Him, so that your strongest desires are to please Him and not a man. **A man can never give you what God can give you.** You will NEVER find complete satisfaction in a man, but you will find it in God.

Your Man is Not Your God

When a woman is vulnerable and desperate and fails to recognize her worth and identity in Christ, she will go to great lengths to get and keep a man. I have both witnessed this and experienced it firsthand. When you want a man so badly, you literally meditate on the thought of him all day long—where he consumes your thoughts and fills all the empty space of your imagination. When you meditate on a man to this degree, you are in effect placing that man in your life in the form of an idol.

The definition of an idol is, "an image or representation of a god used as an object of worship." Do you currently find yourself using a man as an object of worship?

The first man I really fell in love with and the value that I gave him, aligns well with this definition. He was my world. He was broke, living at home with his mamma, had no clear sense of direction for his life, but I worshipped the ground he walked on because my feelings for him overshadowed my reality. I thought the most important thing in the world was being with him because he was constantly expressing his love for me. Anything that threatened the idea of him being my forever I balked at, and I went through great lengths to prove my commitment and my love for him. But, because I gave him all of my time and my emotional and spiritual energy, when things didn't work out, I completely lost it. I didn't think my life was worth living any longer. Here is one of my journal entries from that time:

> *It's over. Me and Landon aren't together anymore. He hates me. I've been thinking about hurting myself because I feel like dying right now. I don't feel like I have anything to live for. I hate myself, and I am the biggest failure that ever stepped foot on this planet. I wish someone would just take me out of my misery.*

Though I did not attempt suicide, I fell into a depression which negatively affected the vision for my life. To be quite honest, I had no vision, which is why I ended up here. To feel as though I was the biggest loser and that my life had absolutely no value or worth outside of this relationship? What a devastating place to be. Even reflecting on what I wrote, brings me mixed emotions. Though I no longer identify with this woman, I know there are plenty of other women who live this reality. Like I said earlier, no man is ever worth dying over! When we give ourselves away, we are left with nothing once the relationship is over. The consequences of that can be devastating.

I cannot stress this enough: **When you put a man in first place, the consequences can be detrimental.** As a matter of fact, you are bordering on dangerous and delusional behavior. I'll take it one step further and say that you are playing with witchcraft. For one, another human being is not humanly capable of ensuring your joy and your happiness are full all the time. Essentially, you are asking that person to be your god and failing to recognize that only The One true God can bring you complete joy. Human beings are full of flaws and full of themselves! We are naturally inclined to put our needs first—not the needs of another person. When you place all your worth and happiness on the outcome of a relationship, you are taking your life out of the hands of

God and placing it into the hands of a flawed and imperfect human being.

More, when you cast all your emotional and spiritual eggs into a severely flawed basket, you are effectively saying, "I am needy, I am desperate, and I am nothing without a man." Is that statement true for you? Are you that detached from reality, considering all the power God has placed on the inside of you, to make a bold declaration like that? I will declaratively state that you, as a daughter of The Most High God, are not needy, desperate, dependent on ANY man, or anything other than God Himself. But, you have to believe that for yourself. So, say it, "I am NOT needy, I AM NOT desperate, and I am not dependent on any man! The only One I seek after in desperation is my Lord and Savior, Jesus Christ."

The Word of God is clear on this point. In I John 5:21it reads, "Little children, keep yourselves from idols (false gods)- [from anything and everything that would occupy the place in your heart due to God, from any sort of substitute for Him that would take first place in your life]. Amen (so let it be). (Amplified Bible, Classic Edition).

Healing and Forgiveness: Keys to Your Breakthrough

So, what do you do when you're ready to move forward and leave your past in the past? How do you move beyond the shame of your broken relationships and the years of regret? The first step is to admit your mistakes and repent.

Ask God to forgive you and to help you live a life acceptable and pleasing to Him. Once you enter a space of humility and repentance, God then has access to mend your heart and to restore what's been broken.

It took much longer than I would've liked to recognize the depth of delusion I was under and to finally come to God and say, "Lord I can't do this anymore. If it isn't what you want for me, I don't want it!" I was steering my own ship for way too long, and as long as I was in control, my life was completely out of control. It took one too many times of bumping my head for me to recognize this. One too many broken hearts to finally let go and let God.

It wasn't until I came to the end of myself that God's true healing took shape. At this point, I was way at the end of my rope. I was desperate for anything but another broken heart. So, God, Who had never left me, began to mend the broken pieces. He ministered to my spirit and my soul and poured His love out on me in ridiculous dosages. Then, something incredible happened. I began to intentionally pursue Him in return. Not just as a provider, a savior, and a deliver, but as a lover and my best friend. **I began to move beyond simply needing God, to actually wanting Him.** That changed everything.

As I embarked upon my season of healing, I stopped old practices, such as listening to love songs that made me desire inappropriate relationships. I cut out movies and television shows which had salacious and scandalous material that in any way pointed to my old life and past relationships. I spent more time in God's Word and in His presence.

I also forgave myself. Since, I was living in darkness and delusion, there was a part of me which didn't know any better. I was blinded by emotion and consumed with the flesh. I also forgave the many men in my life who I felt had let me down. That was a process. I needed to forgive both men that I was romantically involved with and men whom I looked up to as protectors and providers. I needed to forgive, so that I didn't walk through the rest of my life with bitterness and festered wounds that would only do damage to my own life and my future prospects for marriage and healthy relationships with other men.

Healing and forgiveness are key to your survival, whether it pertains to relationships or not. **Holding a grudge and remaining broken destroys the momentum of your life.** It's like experiencing a perpetual Groundhog Day. There is no forward movement. That's not the kind of life you want to live. That's not the kind of life God has called you to live.

Be completely whole, so you can be ready to embrace the call of God on your life. God is drawing you near to Him. He is calling you to return home.

A man can never give you what God can give you.

Return to Your First Love

Do you remember the moment when you first fell in love with God? I mean, really fell in love with Him. That moment where you first experienced the authenticity and the totality of His love? Where you truly experienced the weight of His glory, and you finally identified with all that He is and all that He wants to be in and through your life?

I recall that moment in my own life. I remember it vividly. I was in my mid-twenties and had simply had enough of trying to do everything in my own power. I was tired of living in sin, and I finally relented. I said, "I give up, God!" I told Him I didn't want to continue to live my life the way I was living it. Void of purpose, void of power, and void of His love. I lived so many years in darkness, and I was thrilled to finally hand over the baton to the Master of my soul. My heart is reflected in my journal entry from October 17, 2006:

> Good evening Father. I just love you so much, Lord. You are everything to me, and I am absolutely nothing without You. I still can't believe all of that time You allowed me to live, serving the devil. You are so merciful. I'm just grateful to be alive today to have the opportunity to be a blessing in someone else's life.

One of the pivotal moments that truly caused me to make this change, was the budding life of my daughter. At the time, she was a toddler, and I began to consider the kind of environment in which I wanted her to grow up. I

106

wanted her to be raised with a firm foundation, so when things were difficult, or if she got into any kind of trouble, she would know where to turn. God needed to have a central role in my life, so He could play a central role in my daughter's life.

It doesn't matter how long you've been living in sin, GOD WILL RELENTLESSLY PURSUE YOU and bring you back home to Him. He won't stop until He gets you. Like a possessive lover, He will pursue you and take captive your heart. He created you to have relationship with Him, and until you get to the place of constant companionship with Him, He will continue to nudge you and remind you of His love. He did it for me, time and time again. Even during my darkest hours, God would send people to speak prophetically into my life. And, I didn't understand it then, but I understand it now. God was preparing me for what was to come. He would drop little nuggets of His hope and His love into my life from complete strangers, telling me I would do great things with my life, that God loved me and wanted to use me in a mighty way. I didn't doubt the words spoken, but I didn't see a path out of my sin because I was a hot mess! But, that didn't stop God from loving me, and that didn't stop Him from coming after me.

God is a loving and just God. He won't force a relationship on you. But, He will consistently pursue you even in your sin. Even while you're fornicating with a man who says he loves you but won't prove his love by waiting on your hand in marriage, God will pursue you. He will still pursue you when you find yourself in bed with a married man, wondering how you ever got to a place of deep despair. And, He will pursue you even more, after your heart has been ripped to shreds by a man who has just finished having his way with you and realizes he doesn't want you anymore.

God's love for you is unconditional! It doesn't matter what you have done. **He will never stop loving you.** Can you say the same about any man you've ever dated? The Father is waiting for your return with outstretched arms. His sincere and heartfelt cry to you is, "Come back to your First Love. I've been here waiting for you. And, I'll be here waiting until the ends of the earth."

Don't keep Him waiting any longer. Give up control. Stop trying to do things in your own strength, pursuing relationships you have no business pursuing, and operating outside of God's will. YOU WILL NOT FIND SUCCESS OUTSIDE OF HIS WILL. John 15:5 says, "I am the vine; you are the branches. If you remain in me and I in you, you will bear much fruit; apart from me you can do nothing." (New International Version). There is NOTHING you will be able to accomplish that will have any lasting value without God. PERIOD.

MAJOR THEMES

- Don't be quick to lay your body down for a man but slow to lay your life down for Christ.
- A man can never give you what God can give you.
- Do not make a man your idol or your place of worship.
- When you put a man in first place, the consequences are detrimental.
- God will constantly pursue you even in your deepest sin.
- Holding a grudge and remaining broken destroys the momentum on your life.

ELEVATION

It's time to move forward from the grief and the pain and let go of any and all unforgiveness. I know you've been hurt because I've been hurt. But, it is impossible to fully move into your assignment and move on with your life while harboring unforgiveness. Write a letter to someone you may need to forgive who has hurt you in the past—an emotionally and/or physically absent father, an ex-husband, ex-boyfriend/lover, or your mother. Who do you need to forgive, so you can move forward? You may choose to give the person your letter, or you can simply do this as an exercise, but write one or more letters before moving on to the next chapter. As you write your letter, ask God to bring His healing to your soul.

Part V: Follow Your Purpose

"Instead of your shame you will receive a double portion, and instead of disgrace you will rejoice in your inheritance. And so you will inherit a double portion in the land, and everlasting joy will be yours." Isaiah 61:7 (New International Version)

I am so thankful God did not allow me to get married prematurely. You've read most of my testimony in this book. The relationship challenges I encountered, the lack of respect I had for myself, and the confusion and delusion I was under. Could you imagine if God allowed me to marry while I was so foolish? My marriage would have been a disaster. I would've been truly unhappy and possibly divorced because I would've gone into my marriage with the wrong motives.

Where are you in your level of spiritual maturity? Are you truly ready to get married? Really give that some thought. Have you gotten your house in order? Are you working toward your goals, living your dream, and cleaning out your closet? Or are you on the rebound, still trying to figure out what to do with your life and stuck on the couch catching up on Empire and Scandal, rather than in your Word learning about how to be the virtuous woman your husband needs and a lifetime of marriage requires? One thing I recommend you do not do—is to keep your life on hold while you're single. **Don't wait to start living your life until you're married. Begin to live NOW.** Identify your purpose and chase after your dreams. **Your happiness and your success are not dependent upon a man or your relationship status.** As I have said before, your happiness, contentment, and absolute fulfillment are only found in having a relationship with Jesus Christ. He is the One who gives your life value, meaning, and purpose.

As our time together comes to a close, I want to ensure you walk away from this book with the full understanding of how special you are to God and how important you are to all of humanity.

As a woman, God created you to be especially unique. He created you to be a nurturer, a comforter, a giver, and a lover. He also created you to be a powerful and necessary force in the world. God created us to be the backbone of humanity. We were the last and most critical aspect of God's creation.

Don't wait to start living your life until you're married. Begin to live NOW.

You will begin to experience the fullness of your identity and truly walk in your purpose once you recognize and fully understand who God has called and created you to be as a woman. You will stop settling for whatever and whomever is available the moment you agree with what God says about you. Then, and only then, will you be ready to be received in marriage. Be honest with yourself. Lay all your fears, frustrations, and insecurities bare. God knows what they are anyway. Begin the healing process, so you can be redesigned into the image and reflection of God Himself. So, you can see what God sees. A woman so beautiful, unique, powerful, capable, and deserving. A woman strategically created to serve a very specific purpose in the earth.

Your Identity is Found in Creation

I want you to understand the identity that God gave to women in the beginning of time. God is extraordinarily intentional. He does nothing haphazardly or as an afterthought. Everything He does is absolutely strategic. The very fact that God created Eve to be the VERY last part of creation was nothing short of incomparable genius.

The first chapter of the book of Genesis provides a detailed account of God's creative activity:

> "In the beginning God created the heavens and the earth. Now the earth was formless and empty, darkness was over the surface of the deep, and the Spirit of God was hovering over the waters." Genesis 1:1-2 (New International Version)

God, in His infinite power and wisdom, created the world. His very last act during these six days was creating humankind. God created Adam from the dust of the ground and breathed the breath of life into his nostrils. After He created Adam, God wanted Adam to have a suitable helper—one just like him—dissimilar to the animals that God had already created for humanity to have dominion over.

> "So the Lord God caused the man to fall into a deep sleep; and while he was sleeping, he took one of the man's ribs and then closed up the place with flesh. Then the Lord God made a woman from the rib he had taken out of the man, and he brought her to the man." Genesis 2:21-22 (New International Version)

God brought a perfectly fashioned person of the opposite sex to Adam whom he immediately identified with. Calling her "bone of my bones and flesh of my flesh," Adam acknowledged that woman was taken out of him and that they were joined together as one flesh.

Adam would not have been able to fully realize his purpose in the earth (Be fruitful and increase in number; fill the earth and subdue it...) (Genesis 1:28) without Eve. How can a man be fruitful and increase in number (bear children) without a woman? It's not possible biologically. God designed it that way. His purpose and plan for humanity today is no different. **A man is not completely walking in his purpose until he is joined together in**

marriage with a woman. God set it up this way in the very beginning.

This is why you are so critical. Man needs you, so he can be everything God has called him to be. The Bible makes this evident:

> Then the Lord God said, 'I see that it is not good for the man to be alone. I will make the companion **he needs**, one just right for him." Genesis 2:18 (Easy-to-Read Version).

I want you to reflect on this. God said the companion he needs. So, why, as women, do we behave as if we desperately **need** a man? God created us to be needed, as a critical component to the total fulfillment of God's perfect will. Go back and read Genesis 2:18 again in the Easy-to-Read Version.

My prayer is that you truly get a revelation on this. Eve was the very last part of God's majestic creation. She was what Adam needed to run this entire, big experiment called earth! There was no way possible for Adam to fulfill his assignment in the earth without Eve. Knowing this, you should be struttin' your stuff and poppin' your collar because man needs **you**!! And, a good man—a Godly man—will recognize this. He will come to the end of himself and relate with his identity in God—knowing that he was created to be fruitful and multiply in concert with you, his rib.

As women, we must stop living in fear—the fear of being permanently alone or not having a man of our own. That is a lie of the enemy. The enemy wants you to believe you don't deserve a good man because you were so promiscuous when you were younger, and you are simply reaping what you have sown. While the enemy is laughing in your face, telling you you're getting what you deserved, Jesus is saying, "I already paid the price for those things. I knew they would happen which is why I laid my life down for you."

Jesus paid it ALL for you. Accept your righteousness, renew your mind to the reality of who you are as a woman, and carry on.

Change Your Aroma

Growing up in a minister's home, the rules that were set for dating and encountering the opposite sex were pretty clear, "Dating is pretty much out of the question, and sex is bad, PERIOD." So, like most teenagers, with raging hormones and fits of rebellion, I went completely buck wild. "Sex is bad? Oh yeah; let me find out how bad this thing called sex really is?" I didn't really know what I was doing when I hit the dating scene because I didn't have much instruction. Why was sex so bad? Telling a teenager not to have sex but not explaining that God created sex to be beautiful between a husband and a wife, and fully understanding the many benefits of waiting, I had to operate from a place of ignorance, and figure it out on my own. The solution was to go buck wild.

I became an extremely rebellious teen—lying about where I was going, secretly dating, and especially confused about love. Many women find themselves in this position as a result of having an absentee father or lack of a close relationship with their own father, which was my experience. Young women need their fathers or father figures to guide them on the relationship path—to show them how a man should treat, respect, and care for them. Without these examples and demonstrations of love, women are left to their own devices.

I started receiving advances from married men when I was twenty-one years old. The first married man who attempted to befriend me was three times my age—I spoke about him earlier—the sugar daddy. The next married man was younger, more attractive, and a minister. I couldn't think of a deadlier cocktail. He was so subtle in his advances, initially at least. He was good friends with my boss and was often at my job, until one day he invited me to his church. I accepted. This was after it became clear to me his intentions toward me were not pure. I visited his church, and after service he introduced me to his wife, who was a very beautiful woman. I thought to myself, "What in the world is this man doing trying to stray away from this dime-piece?" This married minister pursued me, and I indulged him. I was considering a big move, and he tried to convince me to stay in town, telling me he could line up a job for me. By God's divine intervention, I ignored him, and continued forward with my plans, knowing he was a disaster waiting to happen, and ended up moving far, far away.

I'm sharing these stories with you because you may find yourself in a place wondering why you always attract the wrong men. Maybe for you, it's not married men. Maybe it's men who are already in committed relationships or are dating multiple women at once. Maybe, the men are deadbeats—whether they are deadbeat dads, deadbeats with no job, or both! Maybe, the men are non-committal—they want the benefits of a relationship (sex, etc.), but not the commitment. Maybe, the men you attract have abusive tendencies. Why do you keep attracting the wrong men?

For the longest time, I could not understand why I couldn't simply meet a man who was void of all of these issues and who could simply love me the way I knew I deserved to be loved. At one point, I thought I had a sign on my forehead that read, "Married men apply within." It was frightening, disgusting, and frankly very disappointing. And, yet, I kept finding myself attracting the wrong men. Until one day, I was having a conversation with some single women from my church, and one sister made a statement that struck a chord which still resonates so powerfully today. She said, **"Until you change your**

aroma, you will always attract the wrong men." It was the most profound statement I had heard in years, and it shook me to my core. This simple statement completely shifted my reality, and it became so clear to me that the issue was not the men (though yes, many of them had issues), the issue was me, myself, and I! I was attracting what I thought I deserved because of the aroma I was giving off. An aroma of desperation, loneliness, neediness, and sensuality.

Like vultures, there are men that will identify the weaknesses in women and prey on them because they themselves have weaknesses. As a woman who struggled for years to see the value of my own life and never felt validated in love, I was an easy target and susceptible to many of the unfortunate encounters that I've already identified in this book. **What and whom you attract is completely within your control.** Take a hard look at the things you do, the places you frequent, the clothes you wear, the mannerisms you make, and the aura you give off. Give thought to the music you listen to, the television shows you watch, and the conversations you're having. If you spend a lot of time listening to music that is heavy on relationships, that talk about needing and wanting a man, that are centered in lovemaking, then guess where you'll find yourself? **What you feed your spirit is what you become.** What are you feeding your spirit?

Really give thought to this because men can smell your aroma—especially a man with ill intentions. He will sniff out your weaknesses and insecurities and take full advantage of you. There is no love in that. You may love the feeling of having him around or how he makes you feel sexually, but the relationship will be unfulfilling and short-lived. There are men who do not begin relationships with the wrong motives. However, if you relax your standards, men will often go there with you. For example, if you say you don't want to have sex before marriage, and then get in the heat of passion and lose control, a man weak in his faith will start taking your clothes off, no questions asked. What man do you know who has a "sometimey" relationship with the Lord, is going to turn down sex? Let's keep it real.

All I'm saying is, don't fall for the okey-doke. You should know what it looks like by now and how it is packaged. You are a very smart woman. If a new relationship comes wrapped in the same package that the old relationship began with (that failed), you need to step back, press pause, and check the price tag. This ain't buy one, get one free. You are a prized package! You are to be loved, cared for, adored, prized, respected, protected, and covered. If these qualities do not exist in your relationship, then why are you in it?

I began the personal journey of changing my aroma once I received the revelation that every time I tried to find love my own way, I failed. Why it took me countless failed relationships for the light bulb to go off, I don't know, but don't judge me! Like most women, I am very forgiving but was detrimentally naive. I believed that each man I dated would be different, and actually love me the way I wanted to be loved. But, until I learned to love myself, I was delusional about what love was. And, so, I had to learn the definition of love:

"Love is patient, love is kind. It does not envy, it does not boast, it is not proud. It does not dishonor others, it is not self-seeking, it is not easily angered, it keeps no record of wrongs. Love does not delight in evil but rejoices with the truth. It always protects, always trusts, always hopes, always perseveres." I Corinthians 13:4-7 (New International Version).

Most of the men whom I dated, had no concept of this definition of love and failed to display any of these characteristics. When I finally took control of my life, my world began to change. I stopped attracting married and trifling men that only wanted one thing from me. I stopped going to the club on Saturday night and then to church on Sunday morning. I stopped wearing short, tight dresses and showing my cleavage, which was a clear sign I was desperate and looking for attention. I had to cut out inappropriate love songs and rated R movies with inappropriate sex scenes so that my spirit was closed to sexual immorality. I had to completely purge my old life and recognize what God made was GOOD! And. that nothing could add to it or take away from it.

I understood God wanted better for me than I wanted for myself, and that his better was bigger than I could ever dream. Once, I began to shed off the old (which is a continual process and does not happen overnight), God began to reveal to me my purpose and prepare me to receive my husband.

Live on Purpose

So, what does it look like to have a changed aroma? What does it require of you to fully give yourself completely over to God, and entrust Him with your heart to give you the desires you want in a husband, in marriage, and in life? It's simply yielding. Yielding yourself over to your Creator and acknowledging He is perfect and knows exactly what He is doing. It's acknowledging God created you for a purpose and with purpose. When you yield, you relieve yourself of the pressure and the confusion that comes when you try to do everything on your own. We trust God with so many other things, why is it so hard for us to trust Him with our relationships?

Trusting God is key to your survival. Once I completely put my trust in God as it pertained to my desire to be married, my world began to change. I started focusing on being the best mother I could be to my daughter and ensuring her needs and her desires were being met. I began to press in to God like I did when I first fell in love with Him years earlier. In so doing, God began to reveal Himself to me in new and absolutely incredible ways. He would strategically place people in my path who would reveal and confirm very specific details about my purpose, and about the calling on my life. Rather than sitting around for another ten years waiting to be married to start living my life, I made the decision to begin to live right where I was.

It's as if God lit a fire in me like he did with Jeremiah, and I could no longer withhold my gifts (Jeremiah 20:9). I laid the ground work for two businesses and launched them both within a year of each other. (I wouldn't recommend this approach, but that's what I did!) All the while, God was blessing me and promoting me on my 9 to 5, allowing His anointing to be favorable toward me in a politically divisive and culturally debilitating environment. Rather than allowing my thoughts to drift toward depression, loneliness, and human companionship, I was intentional about seeking first the Kingdom of God and His righteousness, so that everything I desired could be added unto my life (Matthew 6:33). I remained in the Word and focused on building my dream. Was it always easy? No. Did I allow my attention and my thoughts to drift from time to time? Yes. Was I always and consistently successful in avoiding all sin? No. But did I sit and wallow in my sin and remain there? Absolutely not! I recognized I was virtuous and worthy of true love, despite my past or present sin. **When you recognize that the anointing on your life is greater than your sin, you will not allow yourself to remain in condemnation—unfruitful and unproductive for the Kingdom.**

You may be familiar with the story of Ruth in the Bible. Ruth was a most honorable woman. The book of Ruth does not provide enough context around the various intricacies of the woman, and the sins and kinds of temptation she fell prey to in her lifetime, but the Bible does make it clear, she was very honorable and lived a life of purpose. She refused to leave her mother-in-law's side despite the fact her husband, her husband's brother and father had passed away. It didn't appear Ruth had anything to gain from remaining with her mother-in-law, Naomi, when she could have easily returned home to be with her own family. But, Ruth was honorable and vowed to remain by Naomi's side to serve and support her.

As a result of the honor Ruth showed Naomi, God strategically positioned Ruth in front of a wealthy field-owner named Boaz. Boaz was a godly man with a gentle spirit who was related to Naomi. Boaz noticed that Ruth was hard at work, gleaning (collecting the leftover grains) in his field, so she could provide for her mother-in-law. Ruth was not actively looking for a husband; she was looking to provide and be of support to her mother-in-law. She was looking to ensure they had food to eat and a livelihood. She was too busy focused on what she believed was her purpose at the time—to honor, care for, and provide for Naomi—than to notice any man watching her while she worked. I hope you caught that.

Because of her faithfulness, God blessed her with another husband in Boaz and honored her by being the woman to give birth to a child (Obed) that became the grandfather of King David—in the lineage of Jesus Christ.

Ruth was found gleaning (working) not fiending. Too many women are so busy fiending for a man and desperate to be in a relationship that they lose sight of who they are and never fulfill their purpose. Don't let this be you. What will your husband find you doing? Will he find you faithfully working toward your goals and your dreams or sitting around on dating apps and websites waiting on him to find you, so he can sweep you off of your feet and carry you away to a two-story home in the suburbs?

Become your best self. Right now. Don't wait for it. You haven't even discovered how incredible you are. You have so much to offer that God wants to reveal to you about you, long before you say, "I do." Trust His timing, and while you wait, focus your attention on building your dream.

Chase Your Dream

Everyone was created with a purpose. If you are alive, God gave you the unique ability to do something no one else on this earth can do. What is your purpose? What is that one thing you'd do for free—that you'd jump out of bed and do every day, no questions asked? So many of us live our lives day after day, performing the same routines, without measuring the weight of our work and whether it is truly tied to purpose. Everything you experience in life—every relationship, every job, every decision, every success, every failure—is tied to your purpose.

"We look at this Son and see the God who cannot be seen. We look at this Son and see God's original purpose in everything created. For everything, absolutely everything, above and below, visible and invisible, rank after rank after rank of angels—everything got started in him and finds its purpose in him." Colossians 1:15-16 (The Message)

So, how do you locate your purpose? Well, what do you absolutely love or what do you absolutely loathe? More than likely, that thing, whatever it is, is connected to your purpose. Purpose is often found in our personal experiences, trials, successes, or setbacks. For example, I have a good friend who experienced kidney failure and ended up requiring a kidney transplant. It was through her journey—filled with many emotional, physical, mental, and financial challenges—that she discovered her purpose—educating, supporting, and empowering others who experience kidney failure. Once she realized there were not enough resources, supports, and information for families to navigate kidney disease, having gone through it herself without the necessary supports and information, she decided to do something about it. Now, she's launched her own non-profit helping families secure the information and resources they need to make important decisions about the kidney transplant process. She not only identified her purpose (supporting others through the trials of kidney disease), but she gave life to her dream (launching her non-profit). Imagine if she would've only identified her purpose but never fulfilled her dream. She'd be like the majority of the world. Everyone is given a purpose but only a small minority of us actually pursue and fulfill the dreams tied to that purpose.

Your dream is directly tied to your purpose. If your purpose in life is to help women take control of their physical health in order to live healthier and happier lives, your dream could be creating a franchised women's health facility that attracts thousands of women from all over the country to facilities which provide wellness training, nutritional services, and exercise strategies that are integrated to improve women's overall quality of life. Your purpose is intangible while your dream is tangible. One is passive, the other is active. You can talk about what God created you to do all day, but if you never execute what He's called you to do, no one benefits. But, both your purpose and your dream are equally important because

Everyone was created with a purpose.

your purpose ignites your dream. You must be able to put language to your purpose before you can realize your dream. One without the other just won't work.

Here's an example of how my own dream gives life to my purpose:

Purpose
My purpose in life is to help women let go of their past, discover their purpose, and pursue their dreams.

Dream
My dream is my business platform, The Dream Doctor, which provides individual and group coaching for women who need support to launch their own platforms in ministry, business, or through a non-profit.

So, let's define your purpose. In the accompanying journal or in your personal notebook, write down what you believe is your purpose in life.

Now, that you have identified your purpose and your dream, it's time for you to go about pursuing it. Chase your dream! Seriously, what are you waiting for? You are now liberated from toxic relationships. There should be no desire remaining for you to be sitting around waiting for a man to put a ring on your finger when there's so much work for you to do, right now. Stop chasing after him and start chasing after your dream. Once you do, everything will start to make sense.

Understand, there is a specific need somewhere that is not being met because someone is waiting on you to give them the gift of your purpose. How long will you keep them waiting?

A Good Thing

> "However, let each man of you [without exception] love his wife as [being in a sense] his very own self; and let the wife see that she respects and reverences her husband [that she notices him, regards him, honors him, prefers him, venerates, and esteems him; and that she defers to him, praises him, and loves and admires him exceedingly] Ephesians 5:33 (Amplified Bible, Classic Edition)

Lord have mercy!!! I gotta do all that?! That was my initial reaction—well to be honest that is still my reaction today when I read the second half of Ephesians 5:33 in the Amplified Classic version. Ya'll couldn't have stopped the verse after "esteems him"? I'm just sayin, lol! The Amplified version always trying to add extra stuff. Haha! In all seriousness, Ephesians 5 paints a vivid picture of the role of a wife in marriage. If you want to be a wife, you should also be aware of a wife's position in marriage—to honor and love your husband above every other person in your life.

Sometimes, as women, we feel as if we're losing something when we put someone else's needs before our own. The truth of the matter is, when your husband is meeting your needs, and you are meeting his—it's a win-win situation. Everyone's needs are being met! A husband needs to feel honored and respected. His pride is on the line. So, don't embarrass your man in front of his friends, family, or co-workers. That will not go over well. And, don't act like you're crushing on some famous man on television or any other man, 'cause that won't go over well, either. Your husband wants to be your number one pick—each and every time. Ask God to help shape you to be the kind of woman your husband needs and that God desires.

Before I bid you farewell on this incredible journey that we have taken to remove our sinful stains and rediscover who God has called us to be as women, my prayer is that you walk away with all the tools necessary to succeed on the journey of marriage.

Marriage is not the end goal. Let me repeat—marriage is not the end all be all. It is not the end of a thing. Rather than looking at marriage as some prize you win as a reward for being successfully single, view marriage as the beginning of something entirely new. It is a completely new experience from everything you have ever encountered. It runs counterintuitive to human nature. In marriage, you give with no expectation to receive. You love when you may not always receive love in return. You often sacrifice your priorities and desires for the good of your spouse, your marriage, and your family. You hold up both ends of the deal at moments when your spouse may have the desire to renege. Marriage requires absolute giving and ultimate self-sacrifice. It's far beyond what you have ever imagined or experienced.

Marriage, however, is also extremely rewarding. The opportunity to build a life with someone who is your best friend, your closest confidant, and your life partner has plenty of benefits. You have someone to share in your life events—both your trials and your triumphs. Someone who considers you, before he considers his own needs. Someone whom you might need to brainstorm or strategize with. Someone to build a movement, a ministry, and/or an enterprise with. Someone to help you fulfill your purpose. Being married is one of the greatest benefits of life.

Know that God will present you before your husband when you are ready. Too often we take the reins out of God's hands and present ourselves to our hopeful husbands because we think we are ready. We've talked about this earlier. Let that go. Trust God's timing. His timing is perfect.

Proverbs 18:22 says, *"He who finds a wife finds a good thing and obtains favor from the Lord." (New King James Version)*. A husband finds you. When he finds you, he will find you not as a woman with a mentality and characteristics of a single woman but with the mentality and characteristics of a wife. What characteristics do you embody? Are you desperately chasing after a man or chasing after your dream? Is your head in the clouds due to your fascination with a man, or is your face in the Word of God as you feed on His promises for your life?

Look, it took me longer than I expected to get to a place of final freedom and confidence in who God created me to be. Now, that I am in this place, there's no place I'd rather be. And, I know because of my devotion, my repentant heart, my sacrifice, and my consistency—I will have a blessed marriage that will bear residual fruit. And, He will do the same for you. Do I deserve it? Absolutely not. I was a hot mess as you've read about in this book. But, God would not be faithful to His Word if He didn't offer forgiveness and redemption. And, if you trust Him, if you wait for His direction, if you remain obedient to your assignment without moving ahead of the plan and taking things into your own hands, and if you ask God to intervene and take away certain desires and replace those desires with His desires, God will give you more than you could ever dream.

Jesus has already presented you with His heart. He gave you His heart when He gave you His life. It's time for you to do the same. Give God your heart. Unlike a man, God will not reject you. He will treasure and care for your heart and present you to your husband at just the right time. God has already written the story of your life. Sit back, listen for His promptings, and allow it to unfold the way He orchestrated it before the beginning of time. He's God. He knows exactly what He's doing. Let Him blow your mind!

MAJOR THEMES

- Don't wait to start living your life until you are married. Begin to live NOW.
- Your happiness and your success are not dependent upon a man or your relationship status.
- As a woman, God created you to be especially unique.
- A man is not completely walking in his purpose until he is joined together in marriage with a woman.
- Until you change your aroma, you will always attract the wrong men.
- What you feed your spirit is what you become.
- When you recognize the anointing on your life is greater than your sin, you will not allow yourself to remain in condemnation.
- Everyone was created with a purpose.
- Your dream is directly tied to your purpose.

ELEVATION

Now that you recognize how much God loves you and how much He plans to give you what you desire in marriage, it's time to live. What are you passionate about?

What are your biggest dreams? What do you hope to accomplish with your life, and what kind of impact do you want to have in this world? Oftentimes, when we enter serious relationships, we lose sight of our purpose. We compromise our heart's desires in pursuit of love. If you're reading this, and you are still single, perhaps it's time for you to start living out your dreams. If you are married and you're reading this, find a way to make room for your passions even while being married. Spend some time over the next month identifying your purpose and writing out your dreams—the things that excite you and give your life meaning. It's time for you to start living on purpose and allow God to present you to your mate in His timing and according to His plan.

Prayers

Prayer of Salvation

Dear God, I thank You for loving me and for creating me in Your image. I acknowledge I need help in my life to be a better person—to be the person you created me to be. I need you to clean up the areas of my life that are not pleasing to you. I need You because I need my life to make sense. I ask you to forgive me of my sins and wash me clean. I accept Jesus Christ as my Lord and Savior. I confess with my mouth that Jesus is Lord, and I believe in my heart that You raised Him from the dead. Thank You for accepting me into the Body of Christ. Thank you for giving me a new life!

Prayer of Rededication

Dear Lord, I need your help out of this space that I'm in. I haven't been living the life you desire. I believe in You, and I believe You have better for me. Change my heart God. I want Your will not my own. I don't want to keep chasing after the wrong things, making the same mistakes over and over and over again. I want a new life. I want to fall in love with You all over again. I want to stay in the secret place with You. I confess all my sins, and I know You are faithful and just to forgive me of my sins and to cleanse me of all unrighteousness. I will trust the process. I will trust the plans you mapped out for me before the world began. Thank you for loving me in spite of my past. I love You.

CONFESSIONS

What you say is what becomes a reality in your life. Speak life and receive life. Speak death, receive death. Confessions, with prayer and meditating on God's Word, are powerful tools to keep you grounded in your faith and on the offensive, rather than the defensive in your faith walk and in relationships. Say these confessions out loud, regularly, to build your faith.

Loneliness

I will not submit to the lie of loneliness. I am never alone. In God's Word, He promises He will never leave me nor forsake me. Every need that I have is in Him, including the need to be loved. Every desire that I have is met by Him, including the desire for companionship. I declare that the fear of being alone will not control my decisions and will not run my emotions. I am never alone.

Identity

I know who I am as a child of the Most High God. My identity is in the One who created me. I do not need a relationship to define me or to validate me. I was created in the image and the likeness of God. I will not compromise my faith to accommodate my flesh or a relationship. God created me to be worthy of true authentic and unconditional love. That is the only love I will accept.

Patience

God knows the desires of my heart, and because I am delighting myself in Him, He will give me those desires. As I trust God for my husband, I will not get weary in waiting. I will not get tired of honoring God with my life, with my body, with my finances, and with my gifts. I will not get weary in well-doing. I trust God, His perfect will, and His perfect timing.

Wife in Waiting

Like Esther, I embody the characteristics of a virtuous woman. I don't entertain gossip and trivial conversations. I am not idle in my business dealings, yet I take ownership in my occupation and in my personal finances. I manage my affairs with grace and integrity, and I keep my mind and my body free from impurities. I devote myself to the things of God and to pursuing my dreams and utilizing my gifts for His glory.

My Husband

Like David, my husband is a man after God's heart. He inquires of the Lord and seeks His guidance on all his affairs. He walks in his heavenly authority as a leader and a king in the earth. My husband puts God first in his finances, his time, and all his decisions. He loves me as his bride like Christ loved the church and gave Himself for it. He is devoted, selfless, generous, strong, and loving.

My Marriage

God will give me beyond what I could have ever asked or imagined in my marriage. Despite my faults and past mistakes, God's plans for me and my marriage are good. My marriage will not be short-lived and result in divorce. My husband and I will be on one accord and keep God in the center of our union. When one or both of us have challenges in our marriage, I will be committed to standing in my faith and believing God for the best outcome. Our marriage will encourage and inspire other singles and married couples to honor God and to live a life equally yoked to the vine.

My Family

My family is blessed. We are walking in the Abrahamic blessing and releasing that blessing into the lives of others with our resources, our talents, and our gifts. We are a family of peace and not strife. We are a family of love and of faith not a family of division and fear. We put God first in every area of our lives. We give to those in need, and we love our neighbors as we do ourselves.

SCRIPTURE

The scriptures I am sharing with you here carried me through some of my darkest moments in relationships. Meditating on God's word became the cornerstone of my life and took me from confusion to clarity—from desperation to my ultimate destination. God's Word has served to strengthen me, sustain my resolve, and increase my desire for His Word all the more. It can and will do the same for you.

Hide this Word in your heart and meditate on it as often as you remember.

He has made everything beautiful in its time. He has planted eternity in men's hearts and minds [a divinely implanted sense of purpose working through the ages which nothing under the sun but God alone can satisfy], yet so that men cannot find out what God has done from the beginning to the end. (Ecclesiastes 3:11 Amplified Bible, Classic Edition)

This Book of the Law shall not depart from your mouth, but you shall meditate in it day and night, that you may observe to do according to all that is written in it. For then you will make your way prosperous, and then you will have good success. (Joshua 1:8 New King James Version)

Now what I am commanding you today is not too difficult for you or beyond your reach. It is not up in heaven, so that you have to ask, "Who will ascend into heaven to get it and proclaim it to us so we may obey it?" Nor is it beyond the sea, so that you have to ask, "Who will cross the sea to get it and proclaim it to us so we may obey it?" No, the word is very near you; it is in your mouth and in your heart so you may obey it. (Deuteronomy 30:11-14 New International Version)

I press on toward the goal to win the prize for which God has called me heavenward in Christ Jesus. (Philippians 3:14 New International Version)

Set your mind on things above, not on earthly things. For you died, and your life is now hidden with Christ in God. (Colossians 3:2-3 New International Version)

You were God's expensive purchase, paid for with tears of blood, so by all means, then, use your body to bring glory to God! (I Corinthians 6:20 The Passion Translation)

Finally, brothers and sisters, whatever is true, whatever is noble, whatever is right, whatever is pure, whatever is lovely, whatever is admirable—if anything is excellent or praiseworthy—think about such things. (Philippians 4:8 New International Version)

Do not be anxious about anything, but in every situation, by prayer and petition, with thanksgiving, present your requests to God. And the peace of God, which transcends all understanding, will guard your hearts and your minds in Christ Jesus. (Philippians 4:6-7 New International Version)

Let us not become weary in doing good, for at the proper time we will reap a harvest if we do not give up. (Galatians 6:9 New International Version)

You need to persevere so that when you have done the will of God, you will receive what he has promised. (Hebrews 10:36 New International Version)

We do not want you to become lazy, but to imitate those who through faith and patience inherit what has been promised. (Hebrews 6:12 New International Version)

Little children, keep yourselves from idols (false gods)— [from anything and everything that would occupy the place in your heart due to God, from any sort of substitute for Him that would take first place in your life]. Amen (so let it be). (I John 5:21 Amplified Bible, Classic Edition)

Instead of your shame you will receive a double portion, and instead of disgrace you will rejoice in your inheritance. And, so you will inherit a double portion in your land, and everlasting joy will be yours. (Isaiah 61:7 New International Version)

Keep and guard your heart with all vigilance and above all that you guard, for out of it flow the springs of life. (Proverbs 4:23 Amplified Bible, Classic Edition)

Make God the utmost delight and pleasure of your life, and he will provide for you what you desire the most. Give God the right to direct your life, and as you trust him along the way you'll find he pulled it off perfectly! (Psalms 37:4-5 The Passion Translation)

About the Author

Dr. Monica Almond's mission in life is to help single women let go of their past, discover their purpose, and pursue their dreams. As the head visionary of Monica Almond Enterprises, Dr. Monica (affectionately known as The Dream Doctor) coaches, motivates, and inspires women to live the life of their dreams as entrepreneurs. As the CEO of ZION Publishing House, Dr. Monica helps independent authors bring their book dreams to reality.

A native of Southern California who grew up a preacher's kid, Dr. Monica earned a bachelor's degree in journalism from Howard University (Washington, DC) and a Doctor of Philosophy degree in educational policy from Claremont Graduate University (CA). Dr. Almond lives in the DC-Metropolitan area where she serves in her church and serves as a champion for humanity.

Ready to Chase Your Dreams?

If you've arrived at this page, you're probably at the point where you're sick and tired of being sick and tired. You're done with leaving your fate in someone else's hands and understand that God designed your life with a specific purpose. Well, you've come to the right place.

I've created a free resource to give you the push you need to start you on your path to your purpose, *9 Steps to Living the Life of Your Dreams*. You can access this free resource by singing up on my website at **www.monicaalmond.com.**

If you're ready to move forward on a specific strategy for a business idea you'd like to launch, you can schedule a free discovery session with me on my website.

To stay connected with The Single Woman's Blueprint movement, and to place a bulk order for book clubs, churches, non-profits, and women's groups visit: **www.singlewomansblueprint.com.**

Whether we connect again in the future or part ways here, I'll be praying for your success in all that you do and standing with you as you begin to walk in your purpose so you can live the life of your dreams!

Affectionately,

Monica Almond, Ph.D., **The Dream Doctor**

About ZION Publishing House

ZION Publishing House is a family-owned publishing company based in Southern California and Washington, DC. ZION helps Christian authors tell their stories by providing an affordable alternative to traditional publishing. Our mission is to maintain a platform that educates and empowers independent Christian authors. We do this by cultivating talent in the inspirational and self-help genres for novice and experienced authors. The path to publishing can be daunting and extremely complex. We take pride in taking our clients by the hand and walking them through the publishing process to ensure they not only have a high-quality product that resonates with the reader, but they understand the many facets of the publishing industry and what it means to be a published author.

If you are a writer looking for an affordable path to high-quality publishing, visit our website at **www.zionpublishinghouse.com** to learn more.

[i] N. Nitsche & H. Brueckner. 2009. Opting out of the family? Social change in racial inequality in family formation patterns and marriage outcomes among highly educated women. Yale University. Accessed on February 20, 2017:
http://citeseerx.ist.psu.edu/viewdoc/download?doi=10.1.1.564.611&rep=rep1&type=pdf

[ii] E. A. Carson. 2015. Prisoners in 2014. U.S. Department of Justice. Office of Justice Programs. Bureau of Statistics. Accessed on February 20, 2017: https://www.bjs.gov/content/pub/pdf/p14.pdf

[iii] (McLanahan, Sara and Jencks, Christopher, P15-21, *Was Moynihan Right?: What Happens to Children of Unmarried Mothers—In Education Next, Spring 2015 issue Vol. 15 No. 2*)

[iv] US Census Bureau: Table 4. Poverty Status of Families by Type of Family, Presence of Related Children, Race, and Hispanic Origin: 1959 to 2013).

[v] *Why Men Hate Church.* Accessed on February 20, 2017:
http://www1.cbn.com/churchandministry/why-men-hate-church

[vi] *The State of Our Unions. Marriage in America 2010. When Marriage Disappears: The New Middle America.* Institute for American Values. University of Virginia: The National Marriage Project. Accessed on February 20, 2017: http://nationalmarriageproject.org/wp-content/uploads/2012/06/Union_11_12_10.pdf

[vii] Definition taken from Dictionary.Com. Accessed on November 27, 2017: http://www.dictionary.com/browse/sugar-daddy?s=t

[viii] National Center for Education Statistics. Fast Facts. Historically Black Colleges and Universities. Retrieved here.

[ix] L.B. Cowman. Edited by James Reimann. 1997. *Streams in the Desert: 366 Daily Devotional Readings.* Grand Rapids, MI. Zondervan.